BILL COX'S
GOLF COMPANION

BILL COX'S GOLF COMPANION

BILL COX
AND
NICHOLAS TREMAYNE

WITH LINE AND HALF-TONE ILLUSTRATIONS

J. M. DENT & SONS LTD
LONDON

Made in Great Britain
at the Aldine Press, Letchworth, Herts
for J. M. DENT & SONS LTD
Aldine House, Bedford Street, London
First published 1969

SBN: 460 03846 x

CONTENTS

CONTENTS

APPENDICES

ACKNOWLEDGMENTS

Permission to reproduce photographs is gratefully acknowledged to the following: Sport & General Press Agency Ltd, 3; Associated Press Ltd, 2, 5; Mr Frank Gardner, 4, 8, 9, 12, 13, 15, 16; Mr Sidney Harris, 6, 18; Central Press Photos Ltd, 7, 14, 19; United Press International Photo, 10; Press Association Photos Ltd, 11; Fox Photos Ltd, 23; Keystone Press Agency Ltd, 17, 21; Action Photos, 20; Pace, Sidcup, 22.

I

ABOUT THE GAME

INTRODUCTION
what is golf?

Golf is comedy and tragedy; conceit and humility; a £5,000 cheque and a half-crown sidestake. But above all golf is fun, and a game that gives pleasure to countless millions all over the world. Its magnetism is irresistible. From the moment that the non-golfer takes a vicious swipe at a stationary ball and completely fails to make contact with it, he is bitten by the golf bug. After all, it's so simple, isn't it? One simply *can't* miss it!

Golf *is* simple, but golfers make it complex.

Golf is versatile. It is a game you can play by yourself, or against an opponent, or it can be a team game where you play against two opponents, or a game you play against a field of opposition, or a game you play just against the course itself. And if you were to play the same golf course every day of your life, every shot and every situation would be different, and each round would be a refreshing change from the last.

Golf gives equal pleasure to everyone. The good player half remembers his good shots, but clearly remembers his bad shots of the round. The poor player, or the beginner, forgets his bad shots and lives in an aura of exultation over the odd good shot he played in a game. This is the shot that gives him hope and brings him running back to the first tee the following weekend.

Golf has no favourites. It humbles the great professional, just as it humbles the highest handicap player. And all golfers receive their share of good fortune.

Golf is companionship and a game of lasting friendships and, being a great leveller of men, knows no social barriers. It used to be a game for the so-called 'upper classes', and golf clubs were considered meeting places for the social set. This is not so today. Golf's addicts are drawn from every conceivable walk and level of life.

Golf is lingering memories of sunny days as you sit in the firelight on a snowy winter's evening. Golf is a drink at the bar after winning the match. Golf is heather and bracken, the smell of fresh-mown fairways, the song of a skylark on a breathless morning, a clap of thunder, pelting rain – golf is all these things.

Golf is ageless. The very young and the very old can meet on the first tee and find the same pleasures in life and in their common game.

You too can grasp a little of the happiness that golf brings. All you have to do is to reach out, and the brotherhood of golfers will make you welcome.

THE GAME WE PLAY

Exactly where or when golf was born isn't certain. Some historians claim that it is a direct descendant of the ancient Roman game of *paganica*, others from the Flemish game of *chole*, and yet more maintain that golf's beginnings were rooted in the Dutch game of *kolven*. But whether or not golf has any connection with these other games, it was in Scotland that it developed into the game we know today.

As far as historians have been able to discover, the first reference to golf came in 1457, when King James II of Scotland, who was leading his country in a protracted war against the English, made the game illegal. Apparently it so enthralled the Scots that they had been neglecting their archery practice! But King James was fighting a losing battle on the golf front, however his war with England was going, and the clansmen continued their frantic efforts to hit a little ball into a hole in the lowest number of strokes.

Golf courses were not designed by the hands of men, but rather by the action of the sea and the wind. The game was played on sandy tracts of useless land along the foreshore of the Scottish coasts. The turf was the natural seaside grass, very different from the carefully tended courses of today. Greens, as such, did not exist, and the hole was dug into the turf simply where it was most convenient to put it. Nobody knows for sure why a golf course has eighteen holes, and this really only became standard during the nineteenth century. Certainly, in the early days, a golf course might have only three or four holes, or if there was room, it might have twenty.

The first golf club was formed in 1754, and this was to have an important bearing on the future of the game in Britain, for the

Honourable Company of Edinburgh Golfers, as they called themselves, drew up the first set of simple rules for playing the game. The Honourable Company played over the links of Leith, but ten years later the centre of golfing interest moved to the little Fifeshire town of St Andrews, where the Society of St Andrews Golfers laid out a twelve-hole course, which in time was to become the hallowed Old Course. They also set down a list of rules which still form the basis of the rules we use today. Eventually St Andrews became an eighteen-hole golf course, and as the Society had become accepted as the ruling body of the game in the latter part of the eighteenth century, this was accepted as the norm for a golf course – although for a hundred years or so there were still to be plenty of courses with odd numbers of holes.

In 1766 the first golf club outside Scotland, Blackheath, near London, was formed, and about this time more and more Scottish courses and clubs were being founded.

Stroke play competitions were unknown, and golf to these early pioneers was simply a matter of pitting their skill against the elements and an opponent on a match play basis. To this end they used four or five rude clubs, nearly all wooden-headed with hickory shafts, and golf balls called 'featheries'. These were made of leather and stuffed with a top hatful of boiled feathers. Their manufacture was a slow and laborious process and, while they could be hit a fair distance, they were inconsistent in flight and liable to split open at any time. And so the game went on until the mid nineteenth century, increasing in popularity day by day, but not really developing a great deal.

The first real breakthrough in the traditional game of golf came in the mid nineteenth century with the development of the 'guttie' ball, the first gutties being produced from gutta-percha packing material. Although the first gutties were nearly as inconsistent as the featheries, they were much cheaper to produce, and very soon all opposition to them was swept away.

It was at about this time, too, that some of the great names of the game started to make their presence felt. Many of them, like Old Tom Morris, had been professional caddies who turned their attentions to playing professionally, and in 1860 the first Open Championship was played at Prestwick. There were eight entrants, and the winner was another great player of the day, Willie Park, with 174 over thirty-six holes. Old Tom finished two strokes behind. These two dominated the game until the late 1860's when Young Tom Morris took up the mantle from his father and the Park brothers, Willie and Mungo.

Young Tom started winning money as a professional at the tender age of thirteen, and won his first Open at the age of seventeen in 1868. It marked the first of four consecutive Open Championship wins for Young Tom in what was to prove a tragically short career. When Young Tom was just twenty-four years old his wife died. He was to survive her by only a few months, time spent in the depths of depression. When he died it was generally accepted that Young Tom Morris had died 'of a broken heart'.

During the last decade of the nineteenth century golf really came of age. British professionals travelled to America and taught the game over there, the St Andrews Golf Club, New York, being founded in 1890. In Britain the game was entering one of the greatest periods of its history. It was to become dominated first by two outstanding amateurs, John Ball and Harold Hilton, and then by J. H. Taylor, Harry Vardon and James Braid, who were to become the Great Triumvirate. They were to win a total of sixteen Open Championships, now played over seventy-two holes, between 1894 and 1914, and were to give the game its biggest boost.

Another factor that accounted for the explosion of golf's popularity was the introduction into Britain at the beginning of this century of the Haskell ball. Haskell, an American, had devised a new ball that felt livelier than the solid guttie and flew with greater consistency. The basic idea was a rubber thread wrapped tightly round a rubber core, the whole thing being encased in a thin rubber cover. It was, in fact, the basis for the golf ball as we know it today.

The new ball was expensive to produce and was not an immediate success with the British die-hards who had been brought up on the guttie. When Sandy Herd won the 1902 Open playing with the Haskell, there were even some who felt that his win was not quite fair. Nevertheless this was the turning-point, for more average golfers suddenly had the thrill of being able to hit the ball much farther and much straighter. From then on golf's popularity increased by leaps and bounds.

Over the years golf clubs themselves had slowly been undergoing a change in design. They were becoming shorter in the head and shorter in the shaft. Many of the woods that players of the mid nineteenth century would have carried were being replaced with irons to do specific jobs. Hickory was still the raw material for the shafts and steel shafts did not become generally used until the early 1930's.

From the turn of the century golf became the game as we know it today, although Vardon, Braid and Taylor would have boggled at the vast industry and monumental prize money now involved in the game.

Golf clubs were formed almost daily, in Britain, America and in the smart holiday resorts of the Continent. Women, despite the handicap of long flowing skirts, invaded Britain's golf courses. Professionals, who had previously played challenge matches for cash put up by private backers, began to play in organized golf tournaments, which today is a complete circuit where there are thousands of pounds to be won.

Britain had taught the world how to play golf, but after 1920 it was a case of the pupil teaching the teacher. From across the Atlantic came men like Walter Hagen and the great amateur, Bobby Jones, to capture the oldest golf titles in the world. They were followed by Gene Sarazen, Denny Shute, Craig Wood and many others. The tables were only turned on

America with the appearance of a young man called Henry Cotton, who won the first of his three Opens in 1934. Who can say what Cotton might have achieved but for the intervention of the war?

After the war came a new breed of great professionals from the Commonwealth, heralded by Bobby Locke from South Africa and Peter Thomson from Australia. The game had suddenly become world wide and the rest of the world was sending its best to take part in the British Open Championship. With them came possibly the greatest golfer of all time, Ben Hogan. He had been near to death in 1949 after a dreadful car accident, and doctors had told him that he would never play again. Hogan was to prove them all wrong, and in 1953 his one burning desire was to show the British public that he was still the greatest in the world. From the way he won that Open Championship at Carnoustie, nobody who saw it could have any doubt whatever that he *was* the best.

Now there are other super-stars, golfers who have made millions from the game – Palmer, Player and Nicklaus – men who are heads of vast commercial empires and who fly themselves from tournament to tournament in their own jet planes.

Golf clubs have developed from long, cumbersome implements into beautifully fashioned and balanced instruments; golf balls no longer explode in a shower of feathers – they are meticulously weighed and measured to thousandths of an inch; the long jackets and knickerbockers have given way to colourful, comfortable sweaters and slacks. It's all a far, far cry from that far-off day when King James II of Scotland banned the game so that his clansmen should practise their archery!

THE OBJECT OF THE GAME

Golf is basically a simple game, and although there are many variations to the way we play, the object is always the same – to get the ball into the hole, at every hole, in the least possible number of strokes. For this reason it is one of the very few outdoor games you can play by yourself, for, if you have no opponent, there is always the challenge of the course itself and the satisfaction of completing it with a good score.

Golf combines power, accuracy, delicacy of touch and good judgment, and these are things that have to be learned by practice and experience if you are to score well consistently.

If you can't get a game with anyone else, don't be afraid of going out on to the course by yourself. It's easy to get slap-happy and not really try, so concentrate on making a good swing at the ball every time and try on every shot. If you can, play under a bit of pressure – it's the only way of toughening yourself up and producing your best shots when you most need them.

While your prime object is to get round the course in as few strokes as possible, there are two basic forms of golf – stroke play and match play. In stroke play events you are usually pitting your skill against a whole field of golfers, and the winner is the man who can produce the lowest score when his handicap is taken off the total. In match play you have only one opponent or one pair of opponents to beat, and the match is decided by the 'holes up' method.

SINGLES

Singles match play is the very essence of golf. It is the hand-to-hand battle with only one opponent. A singles match can either be played on level terms or on handicap.

Golf is the only game where players of different ability can fight a game out successfully, because the handicapping system works well. When a player joins a club for the first time, he returns three signed cards. The average of his three scores is then calculated and the *standard scratch score* of the course subtracted (this is the score that the first-class golfer would be expected to produce over that particular course consistently and every golf course has been so rated). Thus, if a golfer returns scores of 90, 91 and 92 over a course with a standard scratch of 72, his handicap would be 19. He can then improve his handicap by playing under it in stroke play competitions. The maximum handicap for men is 24, and 36 for women.

In singles match play the number of strokes given by one player to his opponent is three-quarters of the difference between their handicaps. For instance, if a 12-handicap man is playing a 16-handicap man, the lower player has to give three strokes at allotted holes. Where the strokes should be given will be marked on the card of the course.

The match ends when one player is more holes up than there are left to play. If a golfer wins the sixteenth to go three up, the match must end there because there are only two holes left.

FOURSOMES MATCH PLAY

In foursomes golf every stroke is played alternately by the two partners. If A and B are playing together and A drives from the first tee, B will play the second shot, A the third, etc., but each player must drive alternately as well, so, whether or not B played the last stroke on the first hole, he will drive from the second tee.

To work out the stroke allowances, each side adds together their two handicaps and then takes three-eighths of the difference. If A is 10 and B 12, making a total of 22, and C is 14 and D 16, making 30, A and B have to give three strokes. Sometimes the difference can work out in fractions, and in this case the allowance is to the nearest stroke. Thus, if the difference should be $5\frac{3}{4}$, the lower partnership would give six strokes, but if the difference was $5\frac{1}{4}$, they would only have to give five.

FOURBALL MATCH PLAY

In foursomes each side only plays one ball, but in a fourball, all four players play their own ball, and the better ball of each side counts. Thus if A and B are playing C and D, and players A and C both make fours at the first hole while their partners both take five, the hole is halved in four.

As in singles, the handicapping allowance is worked out on three-quarters of the difference, the lowest member of the four giving strokes to the other three. If A is 10 handicap, B is 12, C is 13 and D is 14, A will give B two strokes (the difference is $1\frac{1}{2}$, but half a stroke counts as one), C two strokes (the difference being $2\frac{1}{4}$) and D three strokes.

MEDAL PLAY

Medal play, or stroke play, as it is more often called, is determined by the total number of shots an individual or a team has taken to complete the course. In the case of an individual player, his companion will mark down the score at each hole, and the total is known as the gross score. When the player deducts his full handicap, this is known as the net score. Most club competitions are decided by net totals, although major events like the club championship may well be dependent on the gross score. If a player completes the course in a gross score of 82, playing off 12 handicap, his net score is 70. If his net total should be less than the standard scratch score, it is quite likely that the handicap committee will reduce his handicap to 11, or even to 10.

In foursome or fourball medal, the principles are exactly the same except that the handicap deduction is half the combined handicap of the pair. If two players of 18 and 20 handicap were playing together, their deduction would be 19.

STABLEFORD COMPETITIONS

One of the most popular forms of competition in British golf clubs is the Stableford. In stroke play competitions, one bad hole can completely ruin a card, but in the Stableford event, you can afford one, or even two, bad holes and yet still return a reasonable card.

Each hole on the golf course is rated by what a first-class player would be expected to do it in. For instance, at a 180-yard hole, the good player would be expected to hit the green with his first shot and then have two putts for a three. This hole would rank as a par three. At a hole of 400 yards, he would expect to find the green in two and have two putts. This would be a par four. But at a hole of 530 yards, only the longest of hitters would be expected to reach the green in two shots, so that the par would be five.

In Stableford competitions points are earned according to your net total at each hole. Two points are earned for a par, one point if you take one more than par, but no points for more than that. Three points are earned for a one under par, or 'birdie', four points for two under par or an 'eagle', and so on.

The scratch golfer would get no stroke allowance at all, and if he were to score 18 consecutive pars, his total would be 36 points. But handicap golfers receive seven-eighths of their total handicap, these strokes being taken at allotted holes. A 16-handicapper would receive 14 strokes, so if he made a par at a hole where he was receiving a stroke, he would have scored a net birdie and earned three points. But if he dropped two strokes at that hole, his stroke allowance would make him only one over par and he would still earn a point.

As you can see from this, it is quite possible to fail to score on a couple of holes, but if you have scored well on your stroke holes, you can still bring in a winning total.

BOGEY COMPETITIONS

Bogey competitions are a slight variation on the Stableford system, and are not now quite so popular at golf clubs as they used to be. A bogey competition is really match play against the course itself, and the player is allowed three-quarters of his total handicap at allotted holes.

If the first hole is a par four and the player makes his four, he is all square with bogey. But if at the second he makes another par and has a stroke there, he goes one up on bogey. Perhaps the third is a long hole and, although he doesn't receive a stroke there, he holes a putt for a birdie four. That makes him two up on bogey. The winner is the player who manages to finish the most holes up on bogey after the full eighteen have been completed. Unlike knockout match play, you do not walk back to the clubhouse if you are more holes down than there are left to play; you hope to improve your position by trying to win back some of those holes. Often a score of all square or even one or two down is good enough to win a bogey competition, so remember that even if you are a hole or two down on bogey other people will be having their troubles on the course.

These are the most usual forms of golf you will come across, and while there are several other types of competition and ways of playing a game they are not in general use in Britain.

If you just play your golf for fun at the club, more often than not you will be playing either singles or fourball match play golf against other members. Obviously a fourball takes longer to complete on a Sunday morning, but is it probably the most popular form of golf simply because it allows more players on to the course at any given time, and also because it gives you the chance of meeting and playing with more people.

Although we have discussed several forms that golf can take, it should be clear that if you are going to succeed at the game, you must try to get the ball into the hole with the least possible number of strokes all the time.

When all is said and done, that *is* the object of the game.

ON STARTING GOLF

So, like thousands of other Britons, you want to take up golf? What is the best way of going about it?

Before going to the expense of buying equipment and trying to join a golf club, it is important to make sure that golf really is the game for you, and to get a proper grasp of the fundamentals of the game. Too many would-be golfers are put off simply because they have tried, unsuccessfully, to hit the ball from the very beginning. They might try a hammer-swing, using all their strength, and then get really disappointed because they can't make any contact with the ball.

The best way of going about your early golfing education is to have one or two lessons from a qualified professional. At least he will give you a proper grounding and help you to hit the ball quite well early on. This will probably give you the confidence and enthusiasm to stick to golf, and the strong desire to improve that motivates all golfers.

Professional tuition is easy to come by, for there are professionals at most municipal golf courses, driving ranges and nearly all golf clubs. You do not need to be a member of a private club in order to receive advice from its professional. During the week particularly, when he is not too busy with his members, the golf club pro will be only too pleased to fix up a lesson for you. Nor is professional tuition expensive – a lesson generally costs a pound to thirty shillings an hour, and it is money that you will consider well spent.

If they are properly used, driving ranges can be of tremendous value to the beginner. Too often people go along to the driving range with one idea in mind: to hit as many balls as possible as far as possible in the shortest possible time. This sort of attitude will never produce a decent, rhythmic golf swing, and the results may turn out to be so frustrating that the desire to play golf is quickly stifled.

However, most driving ranges have a professional staff on hand to give lessons, and in many ways these ranges are ideal practice areas for the new golfer. He is not likely to hit anybody else, he has targets to aim at, and he is not making a nuisance of himself on a busy golf course. Such is the popularity of the driving range that these expensive installations are springing up all over Britain. Some of them are simply mats laid out on a field into which you hit balls, but the more sophisticated ranges have heated bays, automatic tees, bars, restaurants, etc.

Driving ranges are not yet universal, and it is only in the last five years or so that they have been built in Britain, the idea originally having come from the United States. But if there is no driving range in your immediate vicinity, it is almost certain that there will be a municipal golf course not very far away. There are about a hundred and fifty of them in Great Britain, the majority being situated near densely populated areas. Many more are either in the planning stage or actually under construction, for it seems that local authorities have only just woken up to the fact that there is a vast army of people who want to play golf, but have no facilities for doing so.

Municipal golf courses are invariably jam-packed at weekends, but the course professional generally has a practice area where he can give lessons, and the majority of players start in this way. A telephone call to your local council offices will tell you where to find your nearest public course.

With so much leisure time these days, and with so many people able to indulge in their favourite pastimes, there is a tremendous premium on facilities, and nowhere is this problem more acute than in golf. There is a shortage of public courses, and this situation has only recently started to improve, while most private golf clubs are full to capacity and are in no position to accept a sudden influx of new members. At most private clubs, particularly in heavily populated areas, there is a waiting list for prospective members.

You may have two or three friends who are already members of your local club, and your eventual acceptance will depend largely on your relationship with these people. It is standard practice nowadays to be nominated and seconded for membership by people who have known you for a few years and know you to be of good standing in the community. Even so, you might not automatically be elected a member, for you will have to go before a selection committee to be vetted. It helps considerably if you can say that you have reached a reasonable standard of proficiency at the game, for most clubs are not very interested in raw beginners who are only likely to clutter up the course and make a nuisance of themselves at busy periods. Thus the majority of golfers start on municipal courses, where for a few shillings a day they can get to know the game of golf properly.

If and when you are fortunate enough to become elected as a member of a golf club, you will find that initially it is quite costly. Naturally golf club subscriptions are a matter of supply and demand. A golf club near London, for instance, is going to be much more in demand than one in Flintshire. Subscriptions in the south of England can be as high as fifty guineas a year, but the average is probably nearer thirty guineas. In more out-of-the-way spots the fees can be as low as eight or ten guineas. Nowadays it is the normal practice to charge an entrance fee when you are elected, this usually being equal to a year's subscription, so, if you are joining one of the plush clubs near London, you can expect to lay out as much as £100 in your first year, the average being £60.

While some golf clubs are run as limited companies, most are run by the members themselves through a series of committees. While this system doesn't always work perfectly, there are usually plenty of people in the club whose specialized business knowledge can be of value to certain committees. The most important committees as far as the average club member is concerned are the Finance Committee, which is responsible for the club's funds and whose duty it should be to keep subscriptions at a stable level; the Greens Committee, whose major concern is the state of the course and which instructs the club's greenkeeper as to work he should carry out on the course; the House Committee, which is responsible for the running of the clubhouse; and the General Committee, which is an amalgam of all the smaller committees and which is presided over by the captain of the club.

Once you have proved yourself a good club member over a few years, you may well be asked to stand for election to one or more of the committees which will give you the opportunity of taking a share in the running of the club for the rest of the members.

Only a few years ago golf club members were widely considered as snobs, and golf clubs were only for the so-called 'upper classes', but the explosive popularity of the game has broken down any social barriers that existed, and golf is now a truly classless game. Once the average working man discovered the thrill of propelling a little white ball into a hole, and also discovered that the game was well within his pocket, golf ceased to become a pastime for a social *élite*, and most golf clubs nowadays have members from every conceivable walk of life.

Most public courses have golf clubs attached to them, and entry requirements are not so stringent as in ordinary private clubs. If you decide to play for a couple of years on a municipal course it is a good idea to join the club that plays over that particular layout. This will give you the opportunity of getting a handicap and also playing a little competitive golf. Somebody who has a handicap has a much better chance of getting into a private club than an applicant who has never had a handicap. It gives the selection committee a much better idea of your standard of golf, and they will consider much more kindly an applicant who can get round the course without being too much of a hindrance to the rest of the members.

Another way to get a little golf over a private course is to travel to the seaside. Many of the coastal golf clubs depend for their revenue on summer visitors, and are only too happy to welcome fee-paying non-members. At most of these clubs you can pay by the day, weekly or fortnightly, so, when the beginner goes on his family holiday, it's always an idea to put his clubs in the back of the car. He should be able to get some golf, usually without paying too much.

At many urban golf clubs visitors are not so readily welcomed, particularly at weekends when the course is already full of members. Often visitors for the day will only be accepted if they have been introduced by a member of the club, or if they have a letter of introduction from the secretary of their own golf club. If you are planning a day out at a strange club, a telephone call to the secretary can often save you disappointment when you arrive.

THE EQUIPMENT YOU NEED

Golfers are prime targets for manufacturers and the wiles of advertising. Even the most cautious of stockbrokers is more than happy to invest in the latest golfing gimmick if he thinks it might knock a stroke off his handicap, and there is nothing most golfers like more than browsing through the contents of the golf professional's shop.

In spite of this, from the mass of golf equipment produced the beginner's basic requirements are relatively small. He needs a few clubs, a bag to carry them in, a sound pair of golf shoes, and a small supply of balls. This can form the basis for any other equipment you may care to purchase as you improve your play.

The most important consideration is the golf clubs themselves. Each club is designed to do a specific job, and a full set comprises fourteen, the maximum number of clubs one player may carry under the rules. The beginner should not think in terms of spending a great deal of money on the full set, half of which he will not be able to use successfully in the first instance, and which may turn out to be ill-suited to his game anyway.

If you have started your golfing education properly, by going to a professional for lessons, he is obviously the best man to help you to choose your clubs. He can see how your golf swing is developing and can judge your physical capabilities better than anyone else. It is part of his job to see that you are fitted out with clubs that suit you for length, weight and shaft flexibility.

The full set is normally made up of four wooden-headed clubs, nine irons and a putter, and the lower the number of the club, the longer it is in the shaft, and the less loft there is on the face. Of the wooden clubs, the driver, or number 1 wood, is the longest club in the bag and has the least loft, normally about twelve degrees. The number 2 wood is about three-quarters of an inch shorter in the shaft and has a couple of degrees more loft on the face. The numbers 3 and 4 woods are again slightly shorter in the shaft and have comparably more loft. Because of the small amount of loft on a driver, you can only use it from the tee when you have a tee peg under the ball. It is designed to hit the ball with the maximum flight, long and low, and to give the maximum amount of run on the ball when it lands on the fairway.

The other wooden clubs are generally used from the fairway when you have a goodish lie and a long shot still to play, although the number 2 wood can be played most successfully from the tee, and its greater loft than the driver inspires the beginner with confidence.

The nine irons range from the 2 iron to the 9 and the wedge. The 2 iron is the longest shafted of the iron clubs, and the small face has little loft. It is designed to punch the ball low and a long way. The 3 iron has a little more loft, the 4 yet more and so on through the bag. The 9 iron is the most lofted club of the ordinary irons, and is designed to hit the ball very high for a maximum distance of about ninety yards. The wedge is slightly different in character to the other clubs, for it has a broad skid sole which will skim through thick grass or sand without any bother, and the steeply lofted face will help to get you out of any kind of trouble.

Putters come in all sorts of shapes and sizes, and choosing the right one is best left to the individual. If you pick up a putter and immediately say: 'Oh yes, I like that one,' then that is the putter for you. You must be able to feel that you can swing it smoothly, that it is well-balanced, and that you have tremendous confidence in your ability to hit the ball into the hole with that particular club.

There are one or two golf clubs that should be left strictly alone until you are quite a proficient golfer. The 2 iron really has no place in the beginner's bag. It is the longest of the iron clubs, so it is the most difficult to time properly, and the lack of loft does not inspire confidence. The wedge, too, requires a great deal of practice and not a little expertise to play it well, and this is a club to which you should graduate after learning to play the 9 iron properly.

I think that seven clubs are quite sufficient for the beginner – indeed, most club golfers would probably score a great deal better if they limited themselves to seven clubs and learned to play each of them well.

My selection would be a number 2 wood, a 4 wood, 3, 5, 7 and 9 irons, and a putter. The 2 wood will give you greater confidence from the tee than a driver, but be careful to select one that is not too shallow in the face. The 4 wood is a wonderful all-purpose club. You can hit the ball quite a way with it – 200 yards if you are powerful – and the ball doesn't necessarily have to be in a good lie; you can even use it out of light rough. More often than not you will probably use a 4 wood in preference to a 3 iron, but it is worth learning how to play this long iron. Although you may hit it much the same distance as a 4 wood, the flight will be lower, which can be particularly useful in a strong headwind. There is nothing more satisfying than cracking a long iron straight into the heart of a green perhaps 190 yards away.

The 5 iron is probably the basic club in golf, and is always popular with beginners. Coming in the middle of the iron range it has a good loft and is not too long in the shaft. It is an easy club to control and beginners find it easy to get the ball into the air with this club. It can be used for full shots, where the average length may be about a hundred and sixty yards, or it can be used to run the ball up to the flag from just off the edge of the green. It can even cope with rough grass, so long as it's not too thick.

The 7 iron, too, is an easy club to use. A little shorter in the shaft than the 5 and with a few more degrees of loft, it is designed to hit the ball quite high with a maximum operational range for the average golfer of about a hundred and thirty yards. This too can be used with a short swing for little running shots round the green, and is an ideal weapon for getting out of moderately heavy rough.

The 9 iron is a real stroke-saving club. Its great loft is perfect for playing those impressive high pitch shots to the green, and also for getting out of bunkers. For most people, a full shot with a 9 iron will travel no more than ninety yards.

Most beginners buy their first set of clubs before they have developed a sound repeating swing. For this reason it is difficult to judge exactly what clubs will be most suitable. As golf clubs can be pretty expensive items these days, costing as much as six pounds apiece and, as you might well decide to dispense with them after a year or so, it is not a bad plan to ask a professional what second-hand clubs he has in stock. Most professionals, particularly at public golf courses, have a wide range of used clubs which have been traded in for a new set once the previous owner has advanced in the game a little.

There is a popular misconception that the heavier the club the further you will be able to hit the ball. This is completely untrue, and one has only to pick up Jack Nicklaus's lightweight driver to see the error of this theory. Jack has no difficulty in booming drives over three hundred yards with this club, which he always has under perfect control.

If you buy clubs that are too heavy, you will find that they are swinging you, rather than you swinging them. You should be able to feel the clubhead at all times through your hands, and to feel that everything is perfectly under control. Most beginners have weak, untrained hands, and will control lightish clubs best.

Shafts come in four degrees of flex: stiff (S), medium (R), whippy (A) and ladies' (L).

Stiff shafts should be left strictly alone by newcomers to golf, and by the vast majority of club members. They are only for experts who have fast swings and very strong hands.

The R shaft is usually the most suitable flex for the majority of male golfers. It is not so whippy that the clubhead flops around all over the place, but it has sufficient whip to kick into the ball and help the golfer get it on its way.

The A shaft has a good whip and might well be the best shaft for somebody with a slow swing and weak hands, or for the over-fifties, who have not a great deal of power at their command. The whippier shaft will help these folk to get the clubhead into the ball faster on impact, and so hit the ball further. These shafts can also be used by the stronger women players, but unless they have powerful hands, women are best advised to stick to the standard L shaft.

Your height does not make the difference to shaft length that you might think, and this can easily be proved. If a man who is six feet two inches tall stands with his hands at his sides, the distance between his fingertips and the ground will be almost exactly the same as a man of five feet nine trying the same experiment. Thus, so long as you are of relatively normal proportions, the standard length shaft suits practically all men. And the same thing applies to women, for ladies' clubs also have a standard length.

If you decide to go in for second-hand clubs, which might cost you anything between a pound and three pounds apiece, check carefully the condition of the grips. If you like the clubs but the grips are shiny and worn, have them changed. It is well worth the little added expense, for even Arnold Palmer can't hit consistently good shots if the club has a tendency to move about in his hands. The grips should feel tacky and comfortable. Some golfers prefer good leather grips, but if you want to replace them on a second-hand set, the rubber all-weather grips are inexpensive and first class to hold.

Having bought your clubs, you will then need a bag to put

them in. Golf bags range from simple canvas 'drainpipes' which you can buy for a couple of pounds, to leather pantechnicons with dozens of pockets, which could cost you sixty or seventy pounds. Obviously a bag like this would be rather silly for your six or seven clubs, and there are plenty of light carrying bags on the market which have capacious pockets for things like waterproof trousers and golf balls. These will cost you something between three and five pounds.

Too many people disregard the importance of golf shoes when they are kitting themselves out, yet, apart from the clubs themselves, these are the most important items. When you consider that a round of golf takes three hours and you are on your feet the whole time, it becomes obvious that you must have golf shoes that are both comfortable and functional. The golf swing demands considerable movement of the feet, which must be able to grip the turf throughout. For this reason, golf shoes are fitted with spikes in the sole, and these spikes must never be allowed to wear down too far; otherwise you will start slipping and sliding.

Golf shoes may be made from leather, rubber, canvas or even from man-made materials these days. My personal opinion is that leather is the most comfortable material, particularly in warm weather and, as with all good shoes, the life is considerably extended by regular cleaning and by inserting shoe trees when they are not in use.

Golf shoes can cost anything from two pounds to ten, but there are some excellent models on the market at about six or seven pounds. It is a false economy to go in for cheap shoes.

Golf ball manufacture is very advanced now by comparison with the guttie-makers' methods of the last century. Every ball is carefully checked for size, weight, compression, and the depth of those all-important dimples. You can be sure that if you take a new ball out of its wrapper and it starts to behave erratically, it is you and not the ball that is to blame.

Why do golf balls have dimples? The answer is simple. As

the ball spins anti-clockwise through the air, the dimples 'grip' the air and keep the ball in flight. If no backspin were imparted, the dimples wouldn't be able to do their job, and the ball would only fly about fifty yards at the very most. Even if we were to produce backspin on a smooth ball, it would fly nowhere near the distance that a dimpled ball flies.

Our golfing ancestors learnt this lesson during the middle of the last century when the guttie ball became universal. At first these balls were quite smooth on the outside, and the golfers found that they had some most erratic and inconsistent habits in flight – abrupt dips and rises, or sudden nose-dives into the rough in front of the tee. But they soon found out that the longer they played with a ball, and the more it became marked and scored by their clubs, the more consistently did it fly.

Eventually the guttie-makers started cutting shallow criss-crosses on the balls, and later special moulds were made. Many patterns were tried when the rubber-cored ball was introduced from America at the turn of the century – there were balls with raised bumps all over them, others with mesh designs. But eventually it was proved that the modern dimple was the most effective pattern and produced the most consistent flight.

A top-grade golf ball costs nearly six shillings. There is no doubt that, in the hands of a good golfer, the top-grade ball performs better than a second-grade ball, but with the beginner there is virtually no difference. Indeed, as they are such expensive items, the new golfer may be well advised to play with cheaper golf balls, for he will find himself losing a lot, and damaging their covers. Most of the ball manufacturers market reliable second-grade balls for about four shillings.

There is one other piece of equipment that, while not vital, can certainly help the beginner a good deal, and that is a left-hand glove. These are specially made from thin, soft leather, and are designed to help you keep a firmer grip on the club. For the new golfer they serve another purpose as well. Hands that are unused to gripping a club can get quite sore as callouses develop and the skin toughens. This particularly applies to the left hand, and the glove gives the fingers good protection.

As far as clothing is concerned, this is entirely up to the individual, but it is imperative that whatever you wear should be loose-fitting and not restrict you in any way. You can't play golf unless you feel comfortable. For protection against the elements, you might invest in a set of waterproof trousers and jacket, but often jackets tend to be restrictive, so be careful to purchase one that has plenty of room.

As your game and your enthusiasm progress, you will no doubt buy many more accessories. When you obtain your first full set of clubs, you will probably decide you need a bigger bag, and then, because the bag is too heavy to carry, you will want a trolley to wheel it round on. There is no end to the amount of golfing gear you can buy, but the items mentioned here are the basic requirements. You will find that it is quite sufficient to start off with and, if carefully chosen, your equipment will help you to play better golf.

THE GOLF COURSE

Golfers are privileged people. Not only do they get immense pleasure out of hitting a golf ball well, but they have the opportunity of doing it in some of the most delightful surroundings in Britain. Even if the golf course is in the centre of a city and surrounded by houses, it is a satisfying oasis of greenery amid the hurly-burly of town life.

Usually the golf course is to be found a mile or two out of town in peaceful and secluded countryside. Golfers would readily admit that, as soon as they step on to the first tee, all the burdens and worries of life drop from their shoulders. How can you think of the pressures of business when you are totally immersed in one of the most absorbing games ever devised, and when there are all the beauties of nature surrounding you?

There is no such thing as a 'typical' golf course in Britain – every one is different. There can be no comparison, for instance, between a parkland golf course, with its lush green fairways and trees, and a seaside course, built largely on quick-draining sand with lofty sand dunes surrounding you and not a tree in sight. The courses are totally different, and they require a totally different technique to play them well. Then there are the heathland courses, with their sandy subsoil, where heather and gorse are the major hazards for the unwary golfer. Each course has its own particular brand of beauty, and the close-mown fairways and well tended greens with the appearance of a billiard table are a tribute to the painstaking care of the green-keeper and his staff.

For a hundred years or so the standard 'round' of golf has been eighteen holes. Clubs that have both the space and finance to support a full course are lucky indeed, but there are also many golf courses in Britain that have only nine holes, and these are played twice to complete the round, sometimes from different tees for the second time to make the holes slightly different from the first nine.

On a well-designed golf course every shot should be a test of the golfer's skill and ability. The drive must be placed carefully on the mown fairway, avoiding any sand bunkers that may have been positioned to catch the mishit shot, and you should always try to put the drive in the best spot to make the second shot as simple as possible. With your second stroke you are faced with the problem of hitting what seems to be an incredibly small target surrounded, more often than not, by a beckoning beach of sand. It is not always the best golfers that win tournaments, but it is nearly always the golfer with the greatest concentration and determination who finishes on top. If you are going to play any golf course well, there must not be one moment's let-up in your concentration, for in that moment you can hit a bad shot that leads to disaster.

Eighteen-hole golf courses can be anything from 5,000 to 7,000 yards in length, but the average is probably about 6,100 yards. The majority of the holes will be between 300 and 450 yards in length. These rate as par fours, because the scratch golfer would be expected to reach the green in two strokes and have two putts to make his four. Then there may be three or four holes of over 475 yards; these rank as par fives because the scratchman would not be expected to reach the green in two every time. There would also be three or four short holes, which might be anything between 120 and 250 yards in length, with the average being about 170. These are par threes, and the top golfer would be expected to hit the green with his tee shot.

There are no hard and fast rules about how many of each different type of hole there should be on one golf course. A course might have as many as six short holes and only two long ones, another might have five long holes and only two one-shotters – it all depends on the space available.

Usually every hole has three separate teeing grounds in operation at any one time. The back tee is generally used only in competitions or by the club's better golfers – for this reason it is often referred to as the 'tiger tee'. A little further forward is the ordinary men's tee from which most friendly games are played, and still further ahead is the ladies' tee, which helps them to overcome the lack of length in their shots.

Teeing grounds are usually large enough for the greenkeeper to mark out only a relatively small area for use at any given time. This means that he can rest the remainder of the tee and seed badly worn areas. If he is to do his job properly, he requires your assistance and consideration. Use only the portion of the tee that is marked for use; this will reduce the amount of wear and tear that he has to repair.

The beginner will find himself going into many bunkers, which the greenstaff may have spent hours carefully raking so that when you go into them your ball should find a reasonable lie. It is only fair, both to the greenkeeper and to those golfers following you, that when you have played your bunker shot you carefully rake over your footmarks and the spot where the ball lay. Some golf courses supply little rakes beside the bunker for this very purpose but, if there are no rakes, your clubhead does the job admirably.

There is no prettier sight that a well-mown, lush green fairway, and there is nothing more unsightly or more heartbreaking to a greenkeeper than a badly scarred fairway with lumps of turf strewn all over it. To play an iron shot correctly you *must* take a divot of turf after the ball, but if you want to be able to enjoy the golf course next time you play it, you *must* press that divot back firmly into position with your foot. Unless it's very dry the grass will take root again and the fairway will not be badly scarred. There is nothing more irritating than hitting a good drive down the middle of the fairway, only to find that the ball has come to rest in somebody else's unfilled divot mark – or was it one you failed to return yesterday . . .? For everybody's enjoyment, make sure you replace your divots. It takes only a moment and is well worth the little effort.

It is on the greens that the good greenkeeper lavishes his greatest care and attention. Golf courses are almost invariably judged by the condition of their greens. A course may have many shortcomings in its design, but all these are forgiven if the greens are well-cut, an attractive colour and the ball rolls truly on them. It must be heartbreaking sometimes for the greenkeeper to inspect his charges after a busy weekend and see the damage that has been caused to his carefully nurtured turf simply because of the carelessness of the golfers.

To play the game consistently it is important that golfers should be able to keep a good grip with their feet on the ground. For this reason golf shoes are supplied with spikes about three-eights of an inch long and these should never be allowed to wear down too much. But these spikes can do such terrible damage to a green through carelessness. If you are not careful to pick up your feet properly it is all too easy to scuff the surface of the green, gouging the turf badly. Walk on the green as little as possible and, if it is not your turn to putt, try to wait off the side of the green.

When you play lofted pitch shots into a green the ball invariably makes a little circular hole in the surface as it pitches. Be careful to repair these holes before you leave the green. Just gently lift the indentation with the sharp end of a tee peg and tap the repaired mark with the head of your putter so that it is level with the rest of the green.

Another piece of carelessness that can cause damage and spoil the enjoyment of other golfers is replacing the flagstick badly after you have holed out. Make sure that you do not touch the side of the hole as you put the stick back into its recess at the bottom of the hole, and be certain that when you leave the green it is not leaning against the rim of the hole. This will leave an indentation which could easily prevent another player's putt from dropping. The flagstick should always be standing straight up – that way it can do no damage at all.

All these little points take only a moment, yet if every golfer faithfully carried them out, the vast majority of Britain's golf courses would be in much better condition, and the greenkeeping staff would have more time to improving them still further. Golf courses are places of beauty; it is in your power to keep them beautiful or to ravage them. Which would give you the greater pleasure?

Golf is the world's fastest-growing sport, and probably television is the greatest factor in this current boom. Non-golfers have had the opportunity of watching the very best in action, and have felt that they would like to 'give it a try'. That is all to the good, and everybody has benefited. But, unfortunately, television has given many golfers a totally wrong impression of the length of time it should take to complete a round of golf. Simply because the world's great professionals, playing for thousands of pounds, contrive to take and interminable length of time over their shots – particularly on the putting green – this doesn't mean that when you are playing for your friend's half-crown on a Sunday morning, you are going to play any better by dawdling round the course. Indeed, it could be definitely detrimental to your game because you haven't got the tournament-toughened concentration that these professionals have.

More and more British golf courses are becoming plagued by the slow-play disease, and the more frustrated one becomes at having to wait on every shot, the less one enjoys the game. Two golfers really ought to be able to complete a singles match in two and a half hours, and they should *never* take more than three hours. Fourballs are largely blamed for the increase of slow play, but it should be possible on an average-length course to complete a fourball comfortably in three hours – and certainly it should never take more than three and a quarter hours. By all means take your time over your shots and plan exactly what you are trying to do – nobody minds that – but, for goodness sake, walk briskly betweeen shots. If you can encourage all your friends to do the same, you will enjoy the game much more, and it will mean that more golfers will be able to use the course at any given time – and, with the shortage of golf courses, as many people as possible should use them.

ABIDE BY THE RULES

The ruling body of golf in Great Britain and throughout much of the rest of the world is the Royal and Ancient Golf Club of St Andrews, which assumed its important role in the game in 1754 when the Society of St Andrews Golfers drew up thirteen rules for playing the game. These became widely accepted at the time and they also became the basis for the innumerable rules that govern the game today.

In America the ruling body of golf is the United States Golf Association.

There is one extraordinary discrepancy between British and American rules of golf which must become resolved before very long. That is, that in Britain the standard golf ball is 1·62 inches in diameter, and 1·62 ounces in weight, but in America the standard and universally accepted ball is 1·68 inches in diameter and 1·62 ounces in weight. For years there has been tremendous controversy over whether the larger ball is so much more difficult to control and whether regular use of it would improve the standard of British golf. That is an argument I do not propose to discuss here, but it is interesting to see how the Americans tend to hit their ball considerably higher than the British professionals hit the smaller ball. This is simply because the fractionally larger surface area forces the ball higher into the air. And when the American ball pitches on to the green, it tends to stop more quickly because there is a larger surface area for the backspin to take effect.

The original thirteen short simple rules have now been expanded to forty-one, each rule having countless sub-sections to cover virtually every contingency. Unlike tennis, cricket or soccer, golf is not played in a small defined area, and each golf course is so different from another that all kinds of different situations can arise. The Royal and Ancient Rules Committee has tried to include every possibility, and in the rare event of there not being a rule to cover a particular incident, or in the more likely event of difficulty in interpreting the rules, it is the job of the Royal and Ancient Decisions Committee to come up with the answer.

Space prohibits printing the entire rules of golf, but any golfer can obtain a handy pocket book of the rules by contacting the Royal Insurance Company of Liverpool. For many years they have published and distributed rule books free of charge as a service to the game.

The rules are complex, but they become simpler to understand if you consider five underlying principles:

1. The ball must be played as it lies.
2. You must play the course as you find it.
3. There is a basic difference between match play and stroke play golf. There are differences in the rules for the two forms of the game and different penalties for infringement of the rules.
4. You cannot move the ball towards the hole without hitting it with a clubhead.
5. A hazard is holy ground, and under no circumstances are you allowed to touch the ground behind the ball with the club at address.

If you remember these five principles, most of the rules are only a matter of common sense, and you will not go far wrong. But is is always a wise precaution to carry a rule book in your golf bag, so that if any dispute arises on the course the matter can quickly be settled.

Here is a brief summary of the rules which are most likely to affect you regularly on the golf course. Remember that this summary is nothing like complete, and you can't rely on it to settle disputes – for that you must refer to the complete rule book. However, this summary may help to give you a general idea of the most important rules:

BALL PLAYED AS IT LIES

You must play the ball as it lies unless the rules allow you to do otherwise.

IMPROVING LIE PROHIBITED

You must not press down anything which would improve your lie; but outside a hazard you may remove loose impediments such as leaves, loose branches, twigs and wormcasts, provided that the ball does not move either during or after their removal. You may not improve your line of play or lie by moving, breaking or bending anything growing, except in fairly taking your stance or making your stroke.

BALL AT REST MOVED

If you move your ball accidentally, you must play it as it lies under penalty of one stroke.

BALL LOST OR OUT OF BOUNDS

If you can't find your ball after looking for it for five minutes or you hit it out of bounds, you must play your next stroke from where you played the original stroke, counting that stroke and adding a penalty stroke to your score (this penalty is known as stroke and distance).

PROVISIONAL BALL

If you think that your ball may be lost, or out of bounds, to save time you may play a provisional ball from the original spot before going forward, and you may go on playing this ball, until you reach the place where the original ball is likely to be. If you then find your original ball you may continue playing it: if, however, it is lost or out of bounds, you may continue with the provisional ball with the penalty of stroke and distance as in the previous paragraph.

Under a recent ruling you are not permitted to play a provisional ball if you think the original ball may be unplayable. If this proves to be so the player may drop under penalty of one stroke, or return to the original position of the stroke and take a stroke and distance penalty.

OBSTRUCTIONS

An obstruction is something artificial erected or placed on the course but does not include fences and walls marking out of bounds. If the obstruction interferes with your play, and is movable, you may move it. If it is immovable, and if your ball lies within two club lengths of it and it interferes with your stance or the swing of your club in the direction in which you wish to play, you may drop your ball two club lengths from the point on the outside of the obstruction nearest which it lay, but not nearer the hole, without penalty.

CASUAL WATER, GROUND REPAIR, HOLE MADE BY A BURROWING ANIMAL

Casual water is any temporary accumulation of water, including snow and ice. Ground under repair is any part of the course so marked, and includes material such as grass mowings piled for removal, even if not so marked.

If your ball lies, or is lost, in casual water, ground under repair or a hole made by a burrowing animal, or if your stance or swing is interfered with by such conditions, you may drop the ball as near as possible to the original spot avoiding these conditions, but not nearer the hole, without penalty.

If this situation arises when your ball is in a hazard, you may then drop in the hazard without penalty, or behind the hazard under penalty of one stroke.

If your ball is on the green and these conditions intervene between your ball and the hole, you may place the ball on the nearest spot avoiding these conditions not nearer the hole.

HAZARDS AND WATER HAZARDS

When your ball is in a bunker or a water hazard you may not, before making a stroke, touch the gound or water with your club in addressing the ball or in any other way, nor may you test the condition of the bunker, except that you may take up a firm stance. You may not touch or move a loose impediment in a hazard.

When your ball is anywhere in a water hazard you may drop it as far behind the hazard as you wish, keeping the spot where it entered the hazard between yourself and the hole, under penalty of one stroke, or you may play another stroke from where you played the original stroke under penalty of stroke and distance.

When your ball is in a lateral water hazard, which means that it is impossible to drop behind as explained here, then you may drop within two club lengths on either side under penalty of one stroke.

THE FLAGSTICK

You may always have the flagstick attended, removed, or held up to indicate the position of the hole, but you must decide on this before you play your stroke; the flagstick is entirely under your control.

If your ball strikes the flagstick when attended, you lose the hole in match play and suffer a penalty of two strokes in medal play. Under a new ruling the same penalties apply if you strike it when it is unattended and you are on the putting surface.

Before you play, you may adjust the flagstick by placing it in its normal upright position in the centre of the hole; you may not adjust it in any other way to suit yourself.

THE PUTTING GREEN

You may clean your ball on the green, but before the first putt only.

You may repair pitch marks on the green, and under a recent ruling you may now step on the damaged area.

If your opponent's ball is on the green and interferes with your play, you may ask him to lift it.

If in match play your ball strikes your opponent's ball on the green, he may replace it or play it from where it lies at his option and you suffer no penalty: but if in medal play both balls are on the green there is a two-stroke penalty for striking the other ball, which must be replaced.

UNDUE DELAY

You must at all times play without undue delay.

THE GOVERNMENT OF GOLF

Apart from formulating and keeping up to date the Rules of Golf, the Royal and Ancient Golf Club is the fountainhead of the game, not only in Britain, but in many other parts of the world.

The grey stone clubhouse that dominates the coastal strip of linksland outside the little Fifeshire town of St Andrews contains the entire history of the game of golf, from the earliest clubs and balls to famous trophies that have been played for in the past. You cannot join this exclusive club unless you are invited by the members. It may sound autocratic, but that is the way it has always been, and there are no signs of impending change.

Keeping abreast of the rules is almost of full-time occupation for the secretary, his staff and the Rules Committee, but even so they find the time to plan and completely organize golf's oldest title – the Open Championship. The Open is always the height of the golfing year, and during the first two weeks of July the British golfing public waits to see which great name is going to be added to the list of winners. And it is *always* a great name, for a 'bad' winner has never come through to take the little jug trophy. Four rounds of golf, over some of the toughest courses in the world, soon seeks out a player's little weaknesses, and it is only the mentally and physically sound who successfully withstand the tremendous pressures to which they are subjected.

By tradition the Open is always played on a seaside golf course, where the wind and dunes take their toll of all but the strongest. Carnoustie, Hoylake, Royal Lytham, Royal Birkdale, Troon and St Andrews itself – these are just some of the great courses on which a great championship is played. They have provided great champions, giants of the game like Vardon, Braid and Taylor before the First World War, Walter Hagen, Bobby Jones, Tommy Armour, Gene Sarazen and Henry Cotton between the wars, and Bobby Locke, Peter Thomson, Ben Hogan, Arnold Palmer, Gary Player and Jack Nicklaus in more recent years.

The Royal and Ancient Club is also responsible for running the British Amateur Championship, which, like the Open, is always played at a seaside course, and the Boys' and Youths' Championships. All this requires considerable financial resources, which indirectly all golf club members pay.

Each country in the United Kingdom has its own national golfing union which levies the members of all golf clubs affiliated to that union. In England, every male member of a club affiliated to the English Golf Union, pays a shilling a year to the Union, which largely goes towards paying the expenses of English international teams, and the salary of the paid secretary. The residue is split up into donations to the Royal and Ancient's championship fund, and such organizations as the Golf Foundation, whose primary object is to spread the golfing gospel among young people. All four countries in the United Kingdom contribute what they can to the Royal and Ancient Club, and it is largely these donations that have made the Open the roaring success that is is.

The prime object of the national golf unions is to run national championships, and also to standardize handicapping as much as possible in their respective countries. This latter object has also been the driving force behind the Council of National Golf Unions which comprises representatives from each of the four national golf unions.

The Open Championship is the only professional event of a major kind in Britain that is not sponsored by commercial concerns, and it is the only major pro tournament that is not run under the auspices of the Professional Golfers' Association. The P.G.A. is to the paid player what the R. and A. is to Britain's amateurs. It even has the right to alter the rules in the tournaments it runs.

Professional golf has come a long way since the days of Old Tom Morris a hundred years ago and today the P.G.A. controls a circuit worth hundreds of thousands of pounds which begins in April and extends through to October. As yet, the prize money is chicken-feed by comparison with tournaments in the United States, where there is a tournament every week of the year, normal prize money being $100,000 with a $20,000 first prize each week. In Britain the average total prize money is nearer £5,000 with £1,000 as first prize. It is only possible for a few leading professionals to make a good living out of playing the game in Britain. For this reason, most of the older tournament golfers combine their playing activities with the duties of being a normal club professional. The turnover on his shop and the lessons he gives to his members make it possible for him to play the circuit during the summer months.

In America the situation is rather different, and nearly all the tour 'regulars' are players exclusively, and many of them have never given a lesson in their lives. Among the younger British professionals, men like Tony Jacklin, Clive Clark and Brian Barnes, this pattern is also developing, and manufacturers are providing the wherewithal for them to play golf all year round. Now, as soon as the British tournament circuit ends, there is an ever-increasing migration to raid the circuits of the world. During our winter, British players with plenty of ambition travel to Australia, New Zealand, South Africa and the Far East. A few are also turning their heads towards America, where the life is tough, but the rewards immense. Tony Jacklin struck gold within four months of going to America, and became the first British golfer in nearly fifty years to win a major American tournament.

The P.G.A. does not only look after the interests of playing professionals since the vast majority of Britain's pros rarely, if ever, play in tournaments. They are faithful servants to a club and its members, and their major concern is helping more people to play better golf and to enjoy the game more. Most professionals are highly regarded by their clubs, and get their just deserts, but if there should be any serious rift between a club and its pro, the P.G.A. might well be asked to step in on the professional's behalf – almost like a trade union.

Fortunately this is a very rare occurrence, and the P.G.A. is left free to organize its tournaments, seek more sponsors and do what it can to help improve the overall standard of British golf.

Unless you reach a standard where you can enter the Amateur Championship or your national championship, you are not likely to have any contact with the Royal and Ancient Golf Club or with your national union. But each county has its own county golf union, and members of affiliated clubs are free to become members of the union on payment of a small annual fee. In this way you can do something concrete for the good of the game, for this money is usually spent on staging county championships and paying expenses for the county team to play against neighbouring counties, as well as paying the bills when your county is acting as host to a visiting team. Most counties also arrange free coaching for promising young players.

Women's golf in Britain is run on much the same lines as men's golf, with the parent body being the Ladies' Golf Union, which is responsible for organizing such events as the British Women's Championship and international matches. In addition, each country in the United Kingdom has its own women's golf association which runs national senior and junior championships.

GOLF AND BIG BUSINESS

Professional golf really started coming of age in the 1920's, when the great Walter Hagen first came to Britain. Hagen enjoyed the best things in life, and if there was a party going on anywhere, you could be certain that the vibrant 'Haig' would be there.

Though a wild, not to say a bizarre character, the colourful Hagen was the first of the 'gentlemen professionals' who had been used to being fêted in his own country. The pre-war professionals had largely been one-time caddies, and were considered of a lower social standing than club members. Hagen was horrified to find, when he came over to play in the Open, that professionals were not even allowed in the clubhouse and were expected to change in a tent that had been erected away from the clubhouse. In disgust, he changed each day in his enormous hired limousine, which in itself was an eye-opener for the British pros. There were more shocks in store for them, for when the 'Haig' won the Open at his second attempt, he handed the cash prize to his caddie! He had only come for the prestige of winning.

Hagen's visits left their mark on the British professionals, for it suddenly occurred to them that a golf professional need not feel that he belonged to a lower social order.

Gradually they started to break down the barriers, and the professional cause was further strengthened a few years after Hagen's first visit, for there appeared on the scene a young man with a public school background who could hold his own in any company, and was more than a match for anyone on the golf course. His name was Henry Cotton, who was to win three Open Championships and be rated one of the finest players in the world, probably the best that Britain has ever produced. By his example, Cotton virtually completed the work that Hagen had accidentally begun.

Until the start of the Second World War professional golf ambled onwards; there was a small increase in the number of tournaments, but the prize money was small, and even the best of the British professionals had to rely largely on their club jobs to keep body and soul together.

When the war ended there was a marked change in the pattern of British professional tournaments. The 1946 Open Championship was won by Sam Snead, the first American to take the title since 1933. In the years before the war, the Americans had been coming over in smaller numbers for the Open, and there was a danger of the title losing much of its prestige: this was completely restored by Snead's win.

Perhaps of more lasting impact on British golf was the arrival of one or two professionals from the Commonwealth countries. Norman Von Nida, the diminutive Australian professional, was never to win the Open Championship, but in those years immediately after the war, Von Nida and the South African, Bobby Locke, who was to win it four times, cleaned up on the British tournament circuit. They were to be followed in the early 1950's by a young Australian with an easy, relaxed golf swing, and an equally easy manner. His name was Peter Thomson, and he has won the Open no less than five times. Probably for the first time the British professionals were seeing the power of dedication and hard work – for although they had the example of Henry Cotton ever present, the average British professional had, until this time, considered golf a game rather than a business.

If further proof was required of the importance of practice and technique, that proof was found at the little Scottish town of Carnoustie in July, 1953. Four years previously, Ben Hogan's slight body had been racked in a car accident that might well have cost him his life. He arrived at Carnoustie with only one desire in mind: to win the Open. He had already won both the U.S. Open and Masters Championships, and victory in the British title would give him a unique triple.

He didn't set out to make himself popular, and was to smile briefly only once, at the prizegiving. Having unmercifully criticized the hallowed Carnoustie course, Hogan then set out to dissect it clinically in practice rounds. While not caring very much for his attitude, the respectful Scots turned out in large numbers to see the 'little ice man' at work. By the time the championship started, there was not a blade of grass on the course that Hogan didn't know by it's first name, and everybody who had seen him knew that there was no golfer alive capable of stopping him from winning the title he wanted so much.

Hogan and the other post-war visitors had brought an aura of business and science to Britain's golf courses, and it was then that the home players realized that they had been left behind. Their ancestors may have taught the rest of the world how to play golf, but now it was the British professionals who had to take notice and try to learn as much as they could.

While Thomson and Locke continued to dominate British golf throughout the 1950's, more and more overseas players were coming over to join them – Trevor Wilkes, Denis Hutchinson, and a small, determined character from South Africa called Gary Player.

In the meantime golf was growing at a tremendous rate in the United States and professionals who did nothing but play golf were becoming fabulously wealthy. Arnold Palmer, who had turned professional in 1954 after a brilliant amateur career, won the 1958 U.S. Masters title, and the world suddenly realized that here was a young man of extraordinary golfing talent. Everybody wanted Palmer, and the claims on his time were so great that he could not possibly cope with them all in addition to his business interests.

Then Palmer met up with a Cleveland lawyer he had known

since college days. His name was Mark McCormack, and a handshake between the two men was all it required for McCormack to take over Palmer's interests in a managerial capacity. Player, too, had reached the top, and after winning the 1959 British Open, he headed for America, fame and fortune. He, too, joined McCormack, and so began one of the greatest stables of sportsmen ever. Within a year or two both Palmer and Player were millionaires, and presidents of countless companies – many totally unconnected with golf.

At the beginning of 1962 Jack Nicklaus turned professional after a sensational career as an amateur. From the start, great things were expected of him, for in the 1960 U.S. Open, he had finished runner-up to Arnold Palmer, and then Nicklaus was a twenty-year-old amateur. The Golden Bear was virtually assured of a millionaire's future when he, too, signed up with Mark McCormack, but perhaps nobody anticipated just how soon he would make his first million dollars. He appeared on the American circuit in January, but had to wait until June for his first victory. It was the U.S. Open, no less.

In 1960 Palmer came to Britain for the first time to play in the Open. He failed to win it by a hairsbreadth, but his presence electrified the British golfing public, particularly as millions were able to watch him in his titanic struggle with Kel Nagle over the last few holes at St Andrews. The age of television had arrived and it was this new development, probably more than anything else, that has created the tremendous boom in golf today.

It was only in the late fifties and early sixties that television companies began to appreciate that in golf they had a spectator sport that was nearly as fascinating to the non-golfer as it was to the regular player. How many people have taken up the game as a result of watching Palmer and Nicklaus booming those immense drives down the fairway?

Suddenly, with television interested in the film rights of golf tournaments, golf sponsors came to the fore more readily, and with a great deal more money in their hands than previously. If television interest should wane, no doubt sponsorship of professional tournaments would decrease as well.

Every year there are more and more golfers flocking to driving ranges and public golf courses, and the waiting lists at private golf clubs are becoming longer and longer. Today there are about a million and a half regular golfers in the British Isles, plus countless occasional players, but there are only about seventeen hundred golf courses for them to play on. Local councils are slowly appreciating the fact that public golf courses are not simply a waste of good building land, but offer a wonderful return on the capital investment. Golf course architects have more work than they can possibly cope with, but finding enough courses for the ever-increasing number who want to play is a problem that will not be solved overnight.

Financiers have found a partial solution by building golf centres, complete with a driving range and a short course, where every hole is a par three. These centres take up far less space than a full-sized course, but eventually customers will want to try their skill on the 'real thing'.

As the game is booming, so are the big manufacturers of golfing equipment. Two of the biggest manufacturers in Britain can afford to pay Jack Nicklaus and Arnold Palmer thousands of pounds a year for the privilege of having these players' names stamped on the back of their clubs. Such companies can afford to finance young British players, paying their expenses to golf all over the world, in the hope that one day they will turn out to be top-notchers and valuable advertising assets. They can bear the loss of nine failures if the tenth turns out to be a winner.

Golf and the golf business are spiralling ever upward, and the sudden surge of interest in the last ten years is the healthiest thing that has ever happened to the game. Long may it continue!

WHO AND WHAT TO LOOK FOR AT TOURNAMENTS

During the course of a golf season many thousands of spectators go along to professional golf tournaments. Some go merely for the excitement and to see the play, others go to try and learn from the masters of the game.

How much you can learn from watching professionals play depends considerably on how advanced you are as a golfer, and also on how young and strong you may be. The low handicap golfer can sometimes pick up tips by watching the pros that might be disastrous to the long handicap player or to the beginner.

But there is one thing that is common to all the first-class players – the way in which they bring the clubhead square and fast into the back of the ball. My own teaching is based almost entirely on the concept that you must bring the clubhead into the ball as quickly as possible with the hands. It is worth studying the way in which the professionals keep their wrists cocked until the very last moment before impact, and how they hit well down on the ball, taking a divot *after* the face has connected with the ball.

The other lesson that can be learned by watching these fellows is the rhythm with which they hit the ball. This doesn't mean that they all hit the ball at the same speed of swing – far from it – but they all have a smooth complete swing without any suggestion of a jerk in it. The golf swing is one complete action, not a series of movements somehow linked together.

If you want to learn something at a golf tournament, study somebody of a similar build to yourself. If you are tall and supple, you might watch young Brian Barnes and try to decide how he gets his great length from the tee. But there is no use watching Barnes if you are short and stocky – your model might well be Dai Rees who, despite his size, has been at the top of championship golf for over thirty years.

You may have cultivated a short, controlled golf swing, in which case you could do no better than watch Bernard Hunt, whose hands never travel past his shoulders on the backswing. If you have a long flowing swing, watch how the full-swinging professionals keep the club firmly gripped and well under control at the top of the backswing.

Perhaps you've had trouble getting out of bunkers, so watch carefully the way the professionals address the ball when they are in sand, and also the speed at which they swing the club – it's astonishingly slow.

If you are consistently hooking or slicing the ball, as often as not the trouble will lie in the way you are gripping the club. Watch how the professionals place their hands on the shaft, and then try it out for yourself. There are very few decent pros about with bad grips, so you can take almost any of them as your model.

Most of the country's top professionals are strong in one particular department of the game. It is tremendously impressive, for instance, to watch David Thomas driving. He is probably the finest driver in the world, matching Jack Nicklaus for length, but hitting more fairways than Nicklaus. Thomas's power comes from an almost incredibly late hand action, and while the average club golfer might not be strong enough to drive as well as Thomas, it will prove to him that the later he can hit the ball the farther it will travel.

The great Irish professional, Christy O'Connor, is an object lesson for anyone wanting to learn how to transfer his weight through the ball at impact, and O'Connor also has a wonderful sense of timing.

Putting is a personal thing, but most of the professionals stick to one or two basic principles, like keeping the head directly over the ball all the time. Some professionals believe in stroking the ball into the hole with a long follow-through, while others give it a short, sharp rap. It might be worth noting which method the most successful putters employ and then experimenting later on the practice putting green.

Notice, too, how well all the professionals use their strong leg muscles to get that little extra power at impact. Club golfers invariably tend to play too stiff-legged, but these boys use their legs to get all their weight through the ball at the right moment.

It can often be difficult to study someone you particularly want to see when he is actually on the course and playing in the tournament – the crowds may obscure him from your view, or he may not hit the sort of shot you want to see him play. The best answer to that is to check what time he is due to tee off, and then walk down to the practice ground about half an hour before his starting time. Almost certainly, he will be there hitting shots, and won't mind in the least if you watch him. If you want to take photographs, this is the place to do it – not on the course, where the clicking of a camera shutter can be the most distracting thing. Cameras have no place on a golf course during a golf tournament.

Don't try to learn too much in one day, otherwise you will only become confused. Set out for the day with one particular thing to watch for, and compare how different players carry out that particular action. Don't simply ape the professional's idiosyncrasies and style – try to work out what it is he is attempting to do. This will often give you the clue to his style and method.

Above all, watch these players' hands. Their livings depend on the strength of their hands and on their hands bringing the clubface fast into the ball. It is their ability to do this that makes them money winners, and it is this ability that makes them so very different from the average weekend player. If you can learn to reproduce their hand action, you may turn out to be a tournament winner too.

FAIR WEATHER OR FOUL

Hardly an Open Championship goes by without the competitors encountering some of the vagaries of the British climate on these exposed linksland courses. It is always this factor that sorts out the men from the boys and ensures that the winner is the best striker in the field during Open week.

More often than not it is a strong wind that the Open competitors have to contend with, and it causes even the most experienced golfers to lose their rhythm. Club golfers generally quake at the knees when they have to play in a high wind, simply because they have not stopped to think how they can turn the wind to their advantage.

Two basic principles apply in windy conditions:

1. Keep the ball as low as possible when playing against the wind.
2. Let the ball fly high on your long shots downwind.

If you move the ball slightly further back towards the centre of your feet, when playing against the wind, and then concentrate on hitting it with your hands, you will find that this produces a low boring flight. When you are approaching the flag, remember that you must hit the ball right up to the hole, as it will stop almost immediately it lands.

Downwind, use more lofted clubs to get the ball into the air and let the wind carry it. If you normally use a driver from the tee, try using the more lofted brassie instead. But on approach shots remember that the ball will not stop as quickly as usual, and if you pitch it right up to the flag, you can expect to see it go bounding right over the green.

Crosswinds invariably cause club golfers a lot of problems,

because they try to 'steer' the ball towards the flag. After a little experience your judgment will soon tell you how much you should aim to the right of the target in a right-to-left wind, or how far to the left in the case of a left-to-right wind. Once having made up your mind, swing away freely, and don't have any second thoughts. Aim for the target you have set yourself (even if it is a bunker on one side of the green or the other!) and let the wind do the rest – let it work for you rather than against you.

The professionals and low handicap golfers have learnt to draw or fade the ball against a crosswind so that it holds a steady line, but I think that the beginner is better advised simply to make allowances for the conditions and to hit the ball with his normal golf swing.

The great danger when playing in a wind is that you try to hit the ball harder and harder until you are lashing at it with your shoulders rather than hitting it with your hands; you then completely lose all the rhythm of your swing. You must concentrate on keeping the whole action smooth and relaxed. Accept the fact that when you are playing into the wind you will not hit the ball quite as far as usual, but remember that your opponent won't either. If you can keep a cool head while all around you panic, you will win. Don't fight the wind; make as much use of it as you can.

Nobody likes playing in rain, but we must accept that we have to sometimes. Waterproof trousers, or, for ladies, a waterproof skirt, keep the lower half of the body dry quite successfully. Many waterproof jackets tend to be restrictive and can spoil the rhythm of your swing, and for this reason a great many golfers refuse to wear them. The alternative is to carry a golf umbrella, but the drawback is that it can make the wrist stiff and tired after a certain period of time, and this could have an adverse affect on your shots. I find that a good thick woollen sweater keeps water out almost as successfully as anything else, and has none of the inconvenience of waterproof clothing.

If you wear a left-hand glove, take it off between shots and keep it in a dry spot – and it's wise to have a spare handy so that when it gets wet you have got a change. Nobody can play if his glove and grips are wet, so keep a piece of dry towelling in your bag to wipe the grips before playing a shot. If your golf bag has a hood, put that over the top of the clubs and this will prevent water from running down the open end of the bag and on to the grips.

Make sure that the spikes in your golf shoes are all in good order; you can't afford to slip or lose your balance.

Many club players lock their clubs away and forget about them when the cold dark days of winter set in, but with a little forethought and preparation there is no reason why you shouldn't play good golf in cold weather.

If the wrists and ankles are warm, in my experience the rest of the body stays relatively warm. I think a windcheater with knitted woollen cuffs, with perhaps a couple of woollen sweaters underneath, is an ideal arrangement, and two pairs of woollen socks should do the trick of keeping your feet warm. The legs are more of a problem, but one trick that is widely used by golfers who play regularly at the seaside is to wear a pair of pyjama trousers underneath your normal golfing slacks. There is no doubt that this really does help to keep the legs warm.

The most important part of the body in the golf swing is the hands, and to hit good shots you must be able to feel the club-head through your hands. 'Feel' and cold hands don't go together, so you must do something to protect them. A good pair of winter gloves is the only answer, taking them off to play your shots, and putting them on again immediately you have played. It is not altogether satisfactory, but the hands shouldn't completely lose their warmth in the moment or two that it takes to make a swing.

Obviously, with so many clothes on, you can't feel as free as you do wearing only a short-sleeved sports shirt, so I suggest that you do not try to make your usual full swing at the ball. Grip the club an inch or so further down the shaft and just try to play with a three-quarter swing, the hands only going back as far as the shoulders on the backswing. This will help you to keep control of the club and keep the shots flying down the fairway. You might well find that, with this simpler swing, you are timing the shots well and not losing any distance.

You can't hope to play good golf shots unless you are relaxed and as comfortable as possible. The climate is sometimes very unkind, but if you prepare for it and make the best of the situation, there is no reason why you shouldn't play to your normal standard.

RABBIT MEETS TIGER

Two old friends recently played nine holes round a well-known South London golf course. Frank was then a 24-handicap player, while Mike had been playing from a handicap of scratch for about three years, and was the local club champion as well as a regular member of his county's team.

Frank had been playing the game for nearly two years and had the basis of a sound swing, although his hands were on the weak side; as a result of this he tried to make up for it by using a lot of body movement. Mike was not particularly long from the tee, but he hit very straight indeed, and had a beautiful putting touch.

The game was arranged for one Sunday afternoon and Frank, realizing that he was a little out of his depth against such a good player, suggested that, instead of playing a match, Mike might help him to improve the general standard of his golf and give him some advice on how to play the course and the shots. This is a true account of this actual game, as told to me by the scratchman.

FIRST HOLE

This is a fairly straightforward par four of 394 yards, with bunkers right and left of the fairway, and two bunkers guarding the front and right of the green.

Mike teed off first and hit a steady shot about two hundred and thirty yards which drew slightly to the left of the fairway at the end of its flight. Frank, probably a little nervous about playing with such a good golfer, was determined to hit an equally good shot, but in his efforts to hit a big drive he unwound his shoulders from the top of the swing, hit the ground behind the ball, and skied his tee shot about a hundred and fifty yards forward, but into the middle of the fairway.

'Relax,' said Mike. 'Your legs were all tensed up, and you were determined to knock the stuffiing out of the ball. Just try to swing smoothly through the ball as you've been taught.'

When they reached Frank's ball, he was still 240 yards away from the flagstick, but the ball was lying well. His immediate reaction was to reach into his bag for a 3 wood. 'What's the object in that?' said Mike. 'There's no way you can hit the green from here, and you run the risk of knocking the ball into trouble with a wooden club. Use a 4 iron and just try to poke it up the middle and out of trouble.' Frank then hit a well-timed stroke about a hundred and sixty yards, which left him with a relatively simple pitch into the flag.

Mike's drive was ideally placed for the second shot. From the left side, he avoided the bunker eating into the green on the right side, and a firmly struck 6 iron left him with a putt of twenty feet for his birdie three.

Frank was not in such a good position, for with his pitch shot from 80 yards, he had to clear the bunker at the front. He swung his 9 iron well enough, but was so anxious about the bunker in front of him that he jerked up his head almost before the clubface had met the ball. It scuttled along the ground, but he was lucky, and the ball ran over the edge of the bunker and struggled on to the front of the green, forty feet from the hole. As he was farther from the hole, he putted first, but left his ball four feet short of the hole.

Mike then putted, aiming slightly to the left of the hole to allow for the slope. His putt just shaved the left side of the hole and finished nine inches past. Frank holed his for a five.

As they left the green, Mike remarked: 'Always give the hole a chance. If I'd read the line properly, mine would have gone in. Your first putt never had any chance.'

SECOND HOLE

This is another par four of 363 yards. The drive is steeply uphill, but the ground levels out at about a hundred and ninety yards. The green is situated on a high plateau with deep bunkers cutting into the right and left. On this day the flag was situated within a few yards of the left-hand bunker.

Mike drove first, his ball flying slightly from right to left and finishing twenty yards over the brow of the hill, on the left side of the fairway. Frank swung the club more smoothly, but was so concerned about whether his ball would clear the first part of the hill that he looked up too soon. The ball flew low into the hillside and into deep rough. He had no choice but to hack it out on to the fairway, which still left him with a shot of one hundred and eighty yards to the green from an uphill lie. 'Take your 4 wood,' said Mike, 'and swing it smoothly. The loft on the face and the uphill lie will make sure that the ball gets up in the air.' Frank followed his mentor's instructions and hit a good-looking shot, never quite on target, which finished in the right-hand bunker.

Mike's was not an easy shot, for from where his drive had finished the flagstick was immediately behind the left hand bunker. 'This is no time for heroics.' he told Frank. 'I'm just going to aim to the right of the flag where there's plenty of open green. Swinging an 8 iron, he played the shot he had nominated about thirty-five feet right of the hole.

'I'm not very good on bunker shots,' admitted Frank, as they walked up to the ball. 'Well, just remember to open the clubface a little, aim for a spot a couple of inches behind the ball, and swing slowly and smoothly through towards the hole. Frank carried out the instructions to the letter, and was thrilled to see his ball fly out in a cloud of sand and settle ten feet from the stick.

Mike narrowly missed his putt again, but Frank knocked his straight into the back of the hole for a five. 'That could easily have been a six or more,' said Mike. 'It just shows you the importance of being able to play these recovery shots well.'

THIRD HOLE

The third is a par five of 516 yards, but has a wide fairway and relatively wide entrance to the green. The only real trouble is bunkers right and left of the fairway at 190 yards to catch the wayward drive.

Frank, encouraged by the wideness of the fairway, swung the club well and hit a drive down the middle between the two bunkers. If he had possessed greater snap in the wrists, the ball would have easily passed the 200-yard marker, for it was well timed. Mike also hit one down the middle, but about two hundred and forty yards.

Frank's second shot presented no real problems, for there was no question of his getting anywhere near the green and there was no trouble in front of him, but in an effort to hit the ball hard, he rolled his shoulders at the start of the downswing and swung sharply across the ball, causing a slicing spin, which carried his ball into the right-hand rough 'You must remember to hit the ball with your hands, Frank, and *not* with the shoulders. That's one of the worst faults in golf, and anything can happen if you start doing it.'

Mike's ball had finished in a deep lush lie on the fairway, and he wasn't happy with the idea of trying to hit a wood. Instead, he played a safe 4 iron down the middle, leaving himself an approach shot from 100 yards.

Frank had been lucky with his lie in the rough, and he thought that he might just be able to reach the green with a 4 wood from that lie. Mike agreed, but the ball did not come out quite as cleanly as they had hoped, and it came to rest fifteen yards short of the putting surface. Mike's 9 iron to the green was a beauty, and dead on target. It pulled up ten feet past the flag.

When Frank walked up to his ball, he pulled a wedge out of

the bag. 'What do you want to play that for?' asked Mike. 'There are no hazards or rises in the ground, and there's plenty of green between you and the hole. I suggest you play an 8 iron, pitch it on the front edge, and let it run to the hole.' But Frank played the shot slackly with his hands, and didn't follow through with his clubface to the hole. The ball bobbled along the ground and only just made the front edge of the green. 'No matter how short the shot,' said Mike, 'you must always play it firmly with the hands.'

Frank's putt from sixty feet ran twelve feet past the hole, and it was still his turn to putt. Having been scared of the speed of the green after his first putt, he then tamely left it an inch or two short in line. 'Give it a chance,' Mike reminded him – and then promptly holed his ten-footer for a birdie four.

FOURTH HOLE

This is one of the most difficult holes on the course, with a ditch running all along the right side of the fairway which has to be carried from the tee. Having negotiated the ditch, the second shot has to be played to a high plateau which is tucked away behind an outcrop of trees.

Mike played the perfect drive at this 396-yard hole, carrying the ditch, but keeping as close as he dared to the right side of the fairway. This opened up the second shot and gave him a line to the green past the trees on the left.

Frank was not so fortunate, and his anxiety caused him to jerk his head up and top the ball into the ditch no more than fifty yards in front of him. As he had not cleared the hazard, he had to drop the ball out on the side of entry and add a penalty stroke to his score. Thus he was playing his third shot while still only fifty yards from the tee. 'Take a 4 iron and try to keep it out to the right,' counselled Mike. 'That will give you the easiest entry to the green.' Frank hit a real beauty, and, determined that the ball shouldn't plop back into the ditch, he made sure that he watched the clubhead and the ball make contact. His ball winged its way down the fairway for more than 170 yards and finished in the perfect spot.

Mike slightly misjudged the length of his second shot. Because it was uphill, it needed to be pitched right up to the flag. In fact, his 7 iron pitched a yard or two short and didn't run on. 'Take plenty of club, Frank; it's further than you think.' Frank played his 4 iron again, and was pleased to see it sailing into the middle of the green. Until Mike advised him otherwise, he had planned to take a 5 iron.

Mike's crisp little chip shot with a 7 iron from a yard or two short of the green, rolled up to within a couple of feet of the hole for a certain par four. Frank laid his first putt dead, and tapped in the next for a six.

FIFTH HOLE

A downhill short hole, with both the tee and the green set amid trees. The ditch that runs along the fourth crosses the front of the fifth green, only a yard or two short of the putting surface. The flag was situated at the front of the green, 172 yards away.

Mike again misjudged the distance, and although his 5-iron shot looked to be dead on the flagstick, it dropped short and into the brook. The tee being set back in the trees, he had forgotten to take into consideration the gentle head breeze that the ball had met when it left the shelter of the wood.

Seeing his friend's mistake, Frank hit a solid 4 wood, right to the back of the green and over all the trouble.

Now it was Mike's turn to accept a penalty stroke but, dropping the ball over his shoulder behind the ditch, he then played a perfect wedge shot which pitched six feet short of the hole and juddered to a halt about eighteen inches past. He played this delicate stroke with the ball towards his right foot and with a very open clubface. Then with plenty of wrist action he cut right under the ball to produced a lofted shot with terrific backspin.

Frank's putt slid three feet past the hole, but he confidently holed the return for his par three, while Mike tapped his in for a four.

SIXTH HOLE

A par five of 483 yards, with a narrow, slightly uphill fairway and cross bunkers at 270 yards. Tightly bunkered green. Breeze slightly against play.

Having won the fifth hole in a three to a four, it was Frank's turn to drive first from the sixth tee – it was his 'honour', as it is called. His swing looked quite good, but his weak hands had not got the clubface square at impact, and the open face caused the ball to curl away into the rough on the right. Mike hit a beauty, with a low boring flight which rolled on and on once it hit the ground. Despite the slight head wind, he was only a yard or two short of the cross bunkers.

Frank's tee shot, which had only travelled about 180 yards, had finished in quite thick rough and he had to be content with hitting a 7 iron out level with Mike's drive. To make sure of clearing the cross bunkers immediately in front of him, he hit a lofted 4 wood which travelled about a hundred and ninety yards. 'If only your hands were a bit stronger, Frank, you'd have reached the green,' said Mike, taking a 2 iron out of his bag. 'Can you get there with that club?' asked Frank. 'If I hit a very good one. But the 2 iron will keep the ball down lower in this breeze and give it more roll than a wooden club. Unfortunately, I've only got a very narrow entrance to aim at.'

Mike hadn't quite got the length and the ball fell short of the bunker guarding the front and ran into it. When they reached Frank's ball, Mike explained how he had played the delicate wedge pitch at the previous hole, and Frank tried to do the same. The ball soared steeply into the air, but he had not pitched it far enough up to the hole, so that it stopped fifteen feet short. Frank then watched carefully as his friend played his bunker shot; he could hardly believe that the club was swung so slowly, yet with sufficient force to go through the sand. Mike's ball dropped twelve feet past the pin, and then spun back two feet as the backspin took effect on the surface of the green. Even so, it left Mike with an unpleasant downhill putt across a right to left slope.

Frank's putt up the hill was much easier, even though it was further away, but because he could not summon up the courage to strike it hard enough, it finished a couple of feet short. Mike barely seemed to set his ball in motion, but the next moment it had careered four feet past. Knowing that it must be struck firmly, he then rapped the return squarely into the back of the hole. A par five for Mike, and a six for Frank.

SEVENTH HOLE

The seventh is a difficult par four of 381 yards, with the drive into a hill which reaches its crest at 200 yards. The hole then dog-legs to the right into a fairly open green.

Mike, having regained the honour as a result of the sixth hole, hit his drive straight down the middle, but it pitched just short of the crest of the hill and didn't roll on. Nevertheless, he could see over the top and had a view of the green 180 yards away. Frank hit a straight drive, but twenty yards shorter than Mike's which meant that he had a long shot from a steeply uphill lie, and with no view of the green. Frank could not get himself set up comfortably, and eventually took a hopeful swipe with his 4 wood, falling back on to his right leg as he hit the ball. It scuttled over the top of the hill for about fifty yards. 'On those uphill lies,' said Mike, 'you should flex the left leg and keep the right leg fairly straight. Then swing with your hands and arms and little body movement; that will help you to keep your balance and hit the ball with the whole of the clubface. As you were falling back, you only managed to hit the top half of the ball.'

Mike hit a 4-iron shot which pitched just short of the green and ran on. Frank too hit a good 4 iron which finished in the middle of the green, and they both two-putted, Frank for a five, and Mike for a par four.

EIGHTH HOLE

The eighth is a troublesome hole, which dog-legs sharply to the right round trees, the point of the dog-leg being at about two hundred yards. The hole then continues slightly downhill to a green completely surrounded by bunkers.

Mike set himself up to fade the ball round the corner with his driver. Using an open stance, with the left foot drawn further back than the right, and putting his right hand well over the shaft so that the clubface would be slightly open when it met the ball, he swung normally. Sure enough, the ball sailed straight for 180 yards and then gently faded round the corner of the trees out of sight. Frank had no idea of equalling this, but he knew that if he was to have any chance of reaching the green with his second shot, he would have to hit one of his very best drives. Concentrating hard on swinging smoothly and watching the ball closely, he thrilled as the ball left the clubhead, for he knew that he had hit the best shot of the round. When he looked up he saw the ball winging its way to the corner. When it pitched, it caught a downslope which further increased its momentum.

When the two reached their drives, they found they were lying side by side, 160 yards from the green. 'That was a great shot, Frank,' said Mike, 'but remember that when you are playing a shot downhill, you need less club than if you were playing the same shot on the level. I think you could use a 6 iron to pitch it over those bunkers.

Still elated by his tee shot, Frank hit a good 6 iron which just cleared the bunkers at the front of the green and ran to the back. Mike played an 8 iron and hit it very much down and through with his hands, to impart the maximum backspin. He pitched in the centre of the green and the ball pulled abruptly to a halt. They both two-putted for par fours.

NINTH HOLE

The ninth hole is a straightforward par three of 179 yards, the only hazards being a ring of sand bunkers round the green.

Mike effortlessly laid a 5-iron shot seven feet to the left of the hole, but Frank, using a 3 iron, was caught in one of the bunkers to the right of the green. His weak hand action had once again been responsible for the clubface being slightly open at impact but, having watched the ease and smoothness with which Mike had extracted himself from sand at the sixth, Frank felt confident of coming out well. Watching a spot two inches behind the ball, he felt that he was almost swinging in slow motion as he brought his sand wedge down and into the sand.

In fact, while he had played the stroke well, he had taken a little too much sand behind the ball so that it dropped twenty-five feet short of the hole. His first putt was near enough to make his four a formality.

Mike was determined to hole his seven-footer for a birdie two, for that would make him one under par for the nine holes they had played. His determination was his undoing: because he struck the ball too boldly, it hit the back of the hole and spun out, hanging tantalizingly on the lip.

Thus Mike had equalled the par of thirty-six, scoring a birdie four at the long third, but dropping a shot at the short fifth. His card included seven fours, a five and a three, and he had played exactly to his handicap of scratch. Frank was delighted, for not only had he learned a great deal, but he had completed the nine holes in forty-five which was three under his handicap.

A FEVER ROUND THE GLOBE

For those of you who are just being introduced to the delights of the golf game, there are millions more all over the world who are just beginning to get the same thrilling sensation of hitting a golf ball sweetly for the first time.

Great Britain has something like a million and a half to two million golfers, and this number is growing every day. It's the same story in practically every continent and every nation. The golf bug has bitten deep.

Golf's main stronghold, not surprisingly, is the United States, where there are an estimated ten million players using over 8,000 courses. The Americans are facing the same problem as we are in Britain – too many golfers for the available facilities. This has led to dreadful overcrowding and the five-, or even six-, hour round of golf.

The average American golf club is a very different thing to its British counterpart. The British golf club is, as its name suggests, generally a *golf* club pure and simple. It is a place to play golf and have a few drinks afterwards, and perhaps a bite of lunch. The lush American clubs are more often genuine country clubs, with facilities for tennis, swimming, horse-riding, and so on. Of course, there is no comparison between the subscriptions, and a fee of $1,000 a year is not at all unusual in the States. The new member might also be asked to buy a share for, say, $5,000 which is negotiable when he wants to leave the club.

If the situation is bad in America, it is even worse in Japan, a country that has fallen for the charms of golf hook, line and sinker. Again, the clubs are most luxurious, and only the very wealthy or the very important people can gain entry. Of the three million people who hit golf balls in Japan, a great many have never even had the opportunity of playing on a proper golf course. They have to be content with hitting balls at a driving range, and many of the rooftops of Tokyo are rigged up with nets into which the Japanese frenziedly hit balls.

The game is expanding at such a rate in Japan that there can be no solution to the problem in the foreseeable future – there simply isn't enough land available to build more courses.

Golf, traditionally a 'bourgeois' game, has even taken a hold behind the Iron Curtain. It was first introduced into Czechoslovakia about the turn of the century, but under Stalinist repression golf was suppressed. Golfers must still have been practising their swings in secret, though, for over the past few years of liberalization, golf has come out of hiding and there are now two eighteen-hole courses, at Karlovy Vary and Marianske Laszny, as well as several nine-hole courses.

The greatest rate of golfing growth is in the Far East, and even Communist China has one or two professionals who embark on the Far East tournament circuit each year. Presumably, if there are professional golfers, there must be one or two golf courses in Red China.

The Far East circuit is eagerly awaited by thousands of fans in Asia who turn out to see both their local heroes and the golfing heroes from Australia, Britain and America. The Far East tournaments are second only to the American events in the amount of prize money that is offered.

Years ago golf was considered a rich man's game and was played by only a privileged few. Today it is one of the most democratic of sports, and certainly the most world wide.

Golf courses have been cut out of thick, steaming jungle; laid down on desert sand, where not a blade of grass grows; and built on the tops of mountains. But it is in Britain where the game began, and it is here that the spiritual heart still exists. Britain's golf courses are the best and most varied in the world, and our climate helps to make them the best kept. Anyone and everyone is free to play here – young or old, rich or poor.

Golf has proved a great leveller of men, and perhaps this makes Britain's golfers some of the best sportsmen and most honest people you could find anywhere. Golf's like that, and that's why we play it.

2

BILL COX, GOLF TEACHER

INTRODUCTION
a job I enjoy

I must make it clear, from the outset, that I do not teach such methods as swinging with a shut or an open clubface, with a flat or with an upright swing, with a shut or with an open stance. I try to have no gimmicks in my teaching and I don't like any exaggerations or getting too far away from orthodoxy unless I consider it necessary for a pupil to play that way to suit his or her individual style, or perhaps in the execution of a certain specialized shot.

It is quite pointless to blind golf pupils with a host of technical or scientific explanations, and I try to give a pupil only a couple of things at a time to think about while he is swinging the club. One of the first things to do is to erase from my pupil's mind some of the many ruinous catch-phrases that have been adopted in golf teaching over the years – phrases like 'keep the head *down*', 'don't sway into the ball' and so on. As we shall see, such pieces of advice have no place in teaching golf, and can, indeed, be most damaging. So often these 'favourite slogans' are the real cause of the patient's trouble and, until the mind is rid of them, there can be little progress.

I believe in a positive approach to the game and hate to burden a pupil with set rules of what not to do. In this instructional part of the book, in which I want to help everyone to improve their golf, I want, as far as possible, to treat the reader just the same as I would anyone who came to me for a lesson at the Fulwell Golf Club.

Without suggesting that the written word is an adequate substitute for the personal touch in teaching golf – and by this I mean lessons from your professional, of course – I believe that all golfers will find a lot to interest them and plenty of practical assistance in this section. I shall try to show you the causes of your troubles, and, in the simplest of terms, tell you how they can be cured. My aim is to help you to play better golf, because if you play better you will enjoy it all the more.

I am often asked whether I get fed up with just teaching golf all day. To many people it seems a very thankless job standing out on the practice ground hour after hour, teaching so many people, some of whom one knows will never make golfers. Every job has its ups and downs, and all of us who work for a living, no matter what we do, enjoy some parts of our job and thoroughly dislike others. Being a golf professional is really not so very different.

Personally, I love teaching, for each lesson presents a different challenge. I get a lot of pleasure and satisfaction from being in a position where I can diagnose a pupil's faults – rather like being a doctor, I suppose – and then being able to suggest the right cure for his particular golfing 'ailment'.

Most of all I like to teach a person who, in his own opinion, is beyond all hope. Sometimes people come to me and say: 'Look, I've tried everything, and I still play so badly. I've come to you as my last hope; if you can't help me to play better, than I might as well give the game up.' This is a tremendous challenge, and one which I really enjoy. Everything possible must be done to save that man from giving the game up. In the end, nobody is beyond redemption who really wants to improve and is prepared to put his back into it; a person's style can be rearranged if he is keen enough to have the transformation made, has a little time, and is prepared to put some hard work in on the practice ground.

It is very satisfying to teach beginners, too, because you can so quickly mould them correctly. You can make them grip the club properly, you can give them good footwork, and gradually you can see that they are getting the idea of it. You can watch the pleasure they get when they start hitting the ball properly and, with the kind of satisfaction that only the teacher knows, you get as much pleasure as they do.

In teaching golf the psychological approach is most important. When a new pupil comes to me, he may be a little nervous at first. Perhaps he has some particular fault, and he wonders what on earth I'm going to tell him to do, and how I'm going to set about attacking his fault. I always make a point of giving this kind of person a nice easy club, a 5 iron for instance, and tell him to have a few swings with it to get the feel of the thing. Once he is concentrating on swinging, he begins to relax. After a few minutes of this, I have nearly always spotted his particular problem and, even though he hasn't yet hit a ball, I can say 'Well, of course, you're slicing,' or 'You're bothered by a hook, aren't you?' This gives the pupil so much confidence when he realizes that his faults are correctly diagnosed before he has even hit a shot. He feels that the teacher really can help him, and that his knowledge of the game must be pretty sound.

During the first few shots he hits, I take mental notes of how he grips the club, the way he places his feet, the position of his hands, where he plays the ball from in relation to his feet. Then I go behind him so that he is swinging between me and the target. From there I can see whether the club is travelling on the inside or the outside groove, whether he is taking it back flat or upright, whether he opens the clubface as he swings back, whether it is square or shut. All this helps to build up an impression of his problems and, just as every swing is different, so every golfer's problems are different.

I use a high-speed camera in a lot of my teaching as this gives a very clear picture of the player's fault. Once a player can actually *see* the fault himself, he usually realizes how it happens and better understands the advice about curing it.

All kinds of people come to me for lessons, from absolute beginners to top international stars – even Ryder Cup and

Walker Cup players. Over many years I have found that the first-class player is much more difficult to teach than the beginner or the average player. His standards are so much higher and his problems are usually more complex than theirs; if it was a fault in the basic structure of the swing he would be able to work it out for himself. If I can't help him to find a lasting solution, he might feel a little annoyed, but if my advice only serves to make him play worse for a spell, I would feel that I, as the teacher, am to blame. He comes to me for advice and I do my best, but I still find the very good player the most difficult pupil.

Of course, every now and then there is the awkward customer who is terribly difficult. He takes on an almost belligerent air; even though he has paid good money to consult me he refuses to accept what I say. In every job and in every walk of life this type of person comes along from time to time, I suppose. Although he will never make a very good player, if he can play even to 20 handicap, he can still get a great deal of fun out of his golf. So I must try as hard to get the best out of this kind of player as any other, even though he has no natural ability. First of all I have to convince him that I know what I'm talking about and then, once I can get him to swing the club and to understand what it is I'm asking him to do, I'm halfway to getting his confidence and he will do as I tell him.

Many professionals don't in the least enjoy teaching; they find it a bore standing on the practice ground for hours trying to make a pupil do something that may come naturally to the pro, but is seemingly impossible to the student. In my opinion the pros who won't teach at any price are missing a lot of fun in their jobs: they will never get the satisfaction of giving great pleasure, they will never feel pride when a pupil wins a club competition or even an open tournament and they will never have the warmth that first playing and then teaching golf has given me throughout my life. I feel sorry for them and can honestly say that if I had to live my life over again, I wouldn't change one moment of it. Golf has been more than good to me and now I feel privileged, in my own small way, to be able to give something back to the game.

If through these pages I can help you to improve your golf, I shall be amply rewarded.

THE 'SECRET' OF GOLF

After forty years of playing, teaching, writing and talking about golf almost every day, I have come to one conclusion: although it may not be very original, I believe it is the key to playing good golf. All the great players' styles vary considerably, but they have one thing in common: they all feel they can control the clubface in the hitting area, particularly at the moment of impact.

If you were to step out on to a golf course during a major championship you could pick out Doug Sanders, Jack Nicklaus, Arnold Palmer, Henry Cotton, Gay Brewer, Gary Player or whoever you like, simply by watching their swings. You can recognize the idiosyncrasies and mannerisms in their styles a mile away. Yet all these great players hit the ball almost perfectly time after time. If you could block the player out of your picture and just watch the ball fly through the air, would you be able to name the player who had hit it? Nobody could.

All these fellows look different: they are built differently, are different ages, have different strengths and their swings are incredibly different from each other. In spite of this, because they all do the same thing at impact, they all achieve the same result – usually the ball travelling like a bullet straight down the centre of the fairway.

There's no doubt that the hands control the clubface and the clubface controls the flight of the ball. The whole of my teaching is based on this one simple principle, although I sub-divide the golf swing into three separate ideas: style, method and impact. When these three are put together correctly, we have the whole, a sound golf swing.

Style can be taught to almost anyone. If I were to get a group of youngsters together who had never held a golf club before, I could very soon give them reasonable styles. Then if I were to put a ball down, some of them with good styles would not be able to hit it at all. Yet the lad who hardly knows one end of a golf club from the other, the one who may lose balance in his efforts to hit it, might well have the ability to bring the clubhead squarely into the back of the ball. This doesn't necessarily mean that he is going to be the best player, but he has that something extra which is difficult to explain, but which I call ball control. Give a lad like this a stick and he'll hit a ball whether it's moving or whether it's stationary. Give him a football and he'll kick it pretty accurately – he'll hit it with the right part of the foot and drive it to the right spot. Give him a putter and he'll hit the ball fairly accurately at the hole. If you then give that putter to another youngster who has no ball sense, although he may *look* right with it, he probably won't be able to put the ball anywhere near the hole.

So this is what all these top tournament players have in common – they are able to feel the clubface coming into the ball. They are able to put the face of the club to the back of the ball on the intended line of flight and at speed. I believe that once the hands begin to control the clubhead, then you've learned more than half of what golf is all about.

I've seen many very stylish swingers of a golf club. Young girls have come to me who have had lessons, and when I watch them swinging I think to myself: 'My word, this is quite a good style.' Yet when I ask them their handicap it may well be 36. Then, as soon as I put a ball down for them to hit, I realize why it is that they are no better than 36 handicap. They've got what may look like a 6, 8 or 10 handicap *swing*, but they've got a 36, or even a 46 handicap *hand action*.

Again, you have most probably watched the fellow you play with at weekends who has a bad grip, a bad style, stands badly to the ball, swings the club round his body in a rather flat plane – he has, in fact, got what I call an 'agricultural' swing – and yet he's able to 'middle' the ball each time. He cracks the clubface into the back of the ball each time and it flies off down the fairway with a satisfying click as it leaves the clubface. You may feel that it isn't fair that with a style like his he can get away with it. You may feel certain that your style is much better, but still he beats you every time. Why?

The answer is simple, and invariably it's the same. You haven't concentrated hard enough on getting the clubface square to the ball. You may have made a good-looking swing, but you left the clubface open and the ball flew violently off into the trees on the right. With your next shot you are probably subconsciously determined not to do the same thing again, so you roll your wrists and away the ball goes over to the left.

If you really knew your hand action you would be able to modify this wrist roll so that you would be able to turn the ball away from being a slice and bring it back on to the fairway – this is what all the top players do.

I don't suppose there is anyone who would deny that the Americans are the best golfers in the world today, and the one thing that to my mind makes them the best is that they all have tremendous ball control. I particularly remember watching Arnold Palmer play in the Open at Royal Birkdale in 1961, and the par on one particular day must have been 40 or 41 for the first nine holes, such was the strength of the wind. Palmer played what must have been some of the finest golf I have ever seen and he went out in 34 shots.

His ball control was nothing short of phenomenal, and I remember that from some tees he hit his 1 iron, keeping the ball a mere six feet off the ground as it bored its way down the fairway. No wind could affect these shots. Even his approaches were kept low under the wind and he left so many close to the hole that he nearly always had a 'holeable' putt. I think he eventually finished in 71 but two of those were penalty shots. The wind was blowing so hard that the sand in a bunker from which he was about to play moved and he very sportingly penalized himself, although nobody had actually noticed the incident.

Jack Nicklaus makes a fascinating study too. After one of his tremendously long high-flying drives, he often pitches the ball into the flag very low with a tremendous amount of backspin to make it pull up in its tracks. There is just a slight difference in his hand action between these two types of shot, and Nicklaus has got it down to a fine art. This is what I mean by ball control.

I firmly believe in hitting down on every golf shot with the hands, the clubhead connecting with the ball first and then carrying on through to take a small divot after the ball. With this type of action, we are hitting the whole of the ball with the centre of the clubface and producing backspin.

We have all been impressed by Arnold Palmer and Jack Nicklaus when they have hit high approach shots to the flag, and the ball has skidded sharply to a halt only a few feet after pitching. 'Ah,' we say, 'just look at the backspin on that!' Quite right. With their downward hitting action and hands firmly in control of the clubface, these fellows do hit that particular shot with backspin.

But when they step on to the next tee and hit low boring drives that fly through the air for perhaps 220 yards and then roll another sixty or seventy yards, many people think that they have hit the shot with top spin. This is absolutely wrong. The only way you can impart topspin to a golf ball is by hitting the top half of the ball, and if you did that it would only scuttle along the ground for a few yards.

Every shot we hit properly is hit with backspin, and in the case of those long drives, it is merely the fact that the player has minimized the amount of backspin imparted to the ball. The longest drives are usually hit fairly low with a slight right to left flight, and it is this trajectory and spin that keeps the backspin to a minimum. The degree of backspin increases with the loft of the clubs.

If you will remember that *every* golf shot has to be hit with backspin if it is to get into the air, it will make learning golf all the easier for you. It will encourage you to hit down on the ball with a delayed wrist action, and I believe this to be one of the great secrets of playing the game.

A great many young players who are desperately keen to improve may have seen the big names on television, men like Palmer, Nicklaus, Sam Snead or Gay Brewer and, having watched the way these fellows hit the ball, they head for the practice ground with one thought in mind – to try to find 'the secret' that these players obviously have. Invariably they pick on a mannerism that their idol may have, but this is not 'the secret'. As I see it, there is only one secret, if secret it is, and that is control of the clubhead at the moment of impact.

The top American tournament player doesn't only try to hit the ball straight. He learns five distinct shots. He learns to hit the ball with fade, where it starts to the left of the target; he learns to hit it with draw, where the ball starts out slightly to the right of the target; he learns to hit the ball low and straight; he learns to hit the ball high and straight; and he learns to hit the 'quiet' shot. This last one is a hand and arm shot, almost a push shot to the flag.

The value of all these shots can be assessed when there's a strong wind, as there often is on the courses where we play our Open Championship. If a player has a 100-yard shot to the flag, for instance, and elects to use a 9 iron, if he doesn't know how to punch the ball in low with this club there's a terrible danger of it being blown right off course. On the other hand, if one is able to keep the ball down to twenty-five or thirty feet and still attack the flag with a 9 iron, quite often the ball will finish near the flag and give a holeable putt. The Americans, who are absolute masters of this shot, hit it with tremendous backspin because the ball is hit very late with a delayed wrist action. The hands lead the clubface in, hooding it and reducing the loft, and invariably a big divot is taken out of the turf after the ball has been struck.

Many players come to me for a lesson and say that 'all' they want me to do is to teach them to hit the ball straight. They don't want any great length, but they do want to be able to hit it perfectly straight. My answer is always the same: if I could teach them that, I'd be a magician; but if I can teach them to hit the ball with a slight draw, and can teach them to hit it with a slight fade; in other words, if I can help them to find ball control, they will soon be in a position to teach themselves to hit the ball straight. Nearly all the great players in the world use either a draw or a fade consistently. Ben Hogan liked a fade, Bobby Locke preferred a draw, Gary Player hits many of his shots with draw, though he does use a fade almost as regularly. Arnold Palmer, of course, is a tremendously agressive player, and I think with his superb ball control he could do almost anything. He could decide which half of the fairway the ball would end up in, but he would not try to hit it straight there. He would try to draw it to the left-hand side of the fairway or fade it to the right side.

There's no doubt about it: if you learn the two basic strokes of draw and fade, you will very soon learn which method you must use in order to hit your straight shot.

THE FIRST LESSON

The very first lesson for a complete beginner is the most important for him. It sets the whole tone of what is to follow and if the teacher does his job properly, it makes the pupil keen to come back again and to learn all he can about the game. But if he starts off wrongly, his interest in golf can easily finish there and then.

The first lesson must be simple, and when the pupil goes away he must feel that he has done pretty well and that with a little more coaching and practice he'll soon be able to get the hang of it. The golf teacher has not done his job properly if the beginner goes away feeling that he's no good, that golf's too difficult for him, and that he'll never remember all the things he's been asked to remember.

I start an absolutely raw beginner off with a fairly lofted iron club, an 8 iron perhaps, and the first thing I teach him is the correct orthodox grip. Any grip he is going to have will feel fairly uncomfortable at first, so he might just as well learn the correct grip at the outset.

Once he's holding the club properly, I ask my pupil to stand with his feet six inches apart and with the toes pointing slightly outwards. I then explain that all that is required now is a simple back and forth action with the hands and arms, allowing the knees to 'give' a little with the movement – the left knee on the backswing and the right knee on the downswing.

At this stage I am not concerned with footwork; simple easing of the feet with no tension at all is quite sufficient. The golf swing is basically just this very simple back and forth movement, with the hands controlling the club all the time. There should be no attempt to do it quickly and the grip should not be tight. Just a gentle squeezing of the fingers is sufficient to keep a good hold on the club.

This back and forth movement is rather like a long putt, or perhaps a shot that's just off the green, so the backswing must be short and controlled. Very soon the pupil begins to find a rhythm and he begins also to synchronize his small amount of hip action with his hand and arm action. The natural desire is to grasp the club and take a vicious swipe at the ball. Every beginner wants to be able to hit it miles, but if the teacher curbs that desire at the outset, the pupil begins to learn an accurate striking swing, so that when I put a ball down and ask him to use the same short simple swing he has been practising, I quite often find that somebody who has never hit a golf ball in his life before can produce quite a good result on this twenty or thirty-yard approach shot.

The golf swing can be built up slowly from this very elementary action. Once the pupil has got the hang of playing this little shot fairly consistently, I give him a 5 iron. With his 8 iron he will only take the club back three feet and bring it through the ball three feet, but with a 5 iron the length of the backswing and the length of the forward swing are doubled, so that the club is taken just below the right shoulder at the top of the backswing, and just below the left shoulder at the finish of the swing.

This swing helps to promote the correct footwork, for now the heels can be raised slightly from the ground, in order to ease the body action, and the knees will bend a little more. The pupil may not even be conscious of doing this, but it helps him to feel comfortable, so he does it naturally. A comfortable golf swing is not always a good golf swing; but a good golf swing is always comfortable. If you don't feel right, or if you're stretching for the ball, your chances of hitting a good shot are very slim indeed.

Gradually, with a lot of practice swinging, the pupil is building up a sound three-quarter swing. He hasn't yet thought about a full shoulder turn and taking the club back to the

1 Old Tom and Young Tom Morris, 'fathers' of modern golf

Golf becomes increasingly popular

2 Television cameras bring first-class golf to millions and create further interest

3 Paying spectators flock to the Piccadilly World Match Play Championship

Interest in first-class golf spreads all over the world

4 Popular Australian golfer Peter Thomson, five times winner of the Open Championship trophy

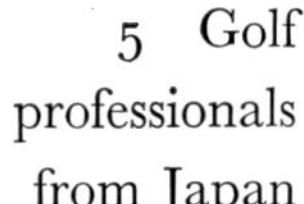

5 Golf professionals from Japan

6 Argentinian golf professional, Robert de Vicenzo; simplicity is the keynote of his style

7 Britain's finest amateur, Michael Bonallack, playing from the rough

8 Britain's most powerful player, David Thomas, hitting *down* on the ball to produce a low boring flight

9 American Jack Nicklaus, perhaps the finest golfer today, hitting through the ball with his hands

10 The hands of a popular golfer, Arnold Palmer

11 Physical training develops Gary Player's golfing muscles

12 Tony Jacklin, winner of the 1968 Jacksonville Open, first British player for nearly fifty years to win in a major American tournament

13 A top British professional for over thirty years, Dai Rees uses a double-handed grip and a flat fast swing

14 Group Captain Douglas Bader, watched here by Bobby Locke, is living proof that everyone can play golf

15 Martin Roesink, perhaps the longest hitter in the world, develops power through a tremendous right leg thrust

16 British international woman golfer,
Pamela Tredinnick

17 The home of golf: the Royal and Ancient clubhouse, St Andrews (building on left)

18 The parkland setting of Stoke Poges Golf Club, Buckinghamshire

19 A driving range, Croydon Surrey

20 The twelfth hole on desolate linksland, Royal Birkdale

21 Henry Cotton gives expert advice on choosing the right equipment from the vast array in a professional's shop

22 The Golf Foundation's junior coaching scheme has done much to make the game popular with younger players

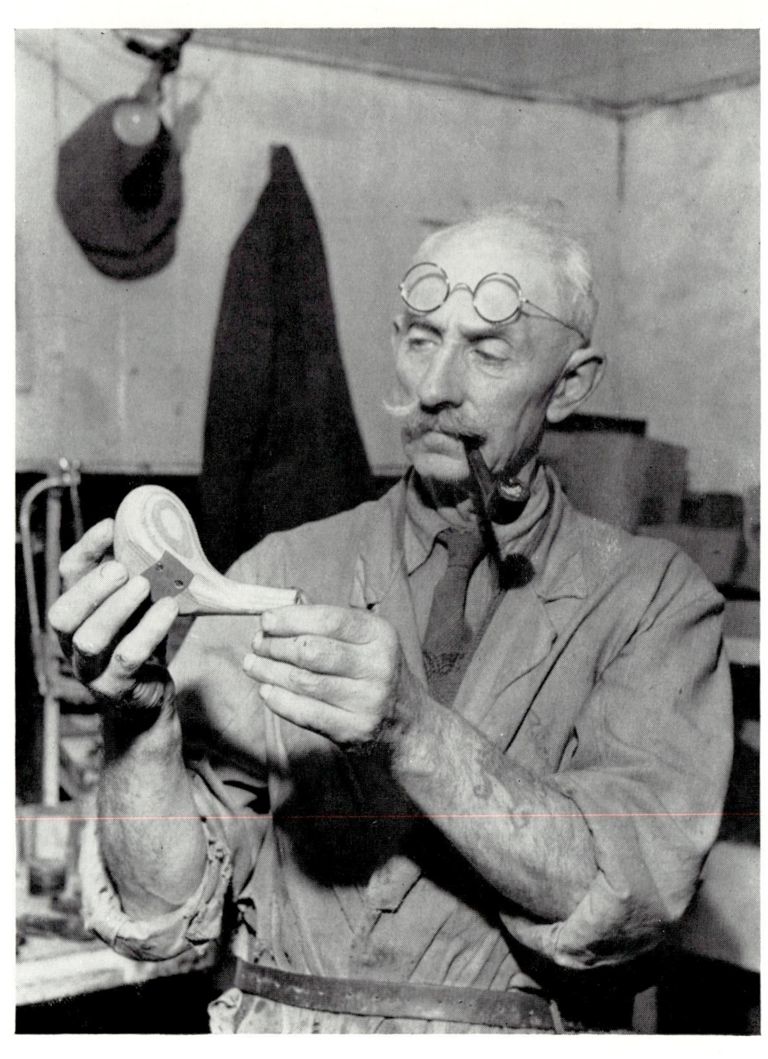

23 A craftsman clubmaker gives a final check to a finished club head

horizontal position at the top of the backswing, but he must appreciate that this three-quarter swing is the basis for all his shots. His swing may be longer or it may be shorter as the circumstances demand, but the way he comes into the ball and goes through the ball, with the hands firmly in control, will be exactly the same on every shot he plays.

It's essential that, in this first lesson, the pupil should not attempt to hit the ball hard; he must *not* try to swing the clubhead fast at the ball. He must learn simple sweeping types of action with no snatch, and no looking forward to see where the ball has gone. The head must remain perfectly still, and the teacher has to drill into his pupil's mind all the time that this is a simple back and forth movement, while watching the ball closely and trying to feel exactly where the clubhead is and how his wrists, hands and arms are working.

Once the beginner feels that he has mastered this elementary swing, he'll start to feel quite pleased with himself. He suddenly finds that he can hit the ball more often than he misses it. When, occasionally, he will really hit one out of the middle of the clubface his hands and arms will thrill to that strange feeling. This is just the kind of encouragement he needs. He has probably watched some of the golf matches on television and seen Gary Player producing tremendously expert little shots from just off the green which run up to within a foot or so of the hole. During his first lesson the beginner won't be aiming at any particular target; he will just be trying to hit the ball with the clubface, but perhaps there may be one or two balls up the practice fairway, and when he reaches the stage of being able to get the ball up into the air and hit it twenty or thirty yards, all these little shots soon land in the same area. Immediately the competition is on, for he has created his own target area to aim at. He may not be a Gary Player, but now he is playing a real golf shot with an object in mind.

What has the pupil achieved in this first lesson? He has learned the correct grip and simple footwork. He has learned to take the club back and forth with no complicated body pivot. Most important of all he has learned that the basic golf swing is a simple one, and this gives him the confidence he so badly needs at this stage of the proceedings. He is not worried about such things as whether he should keep his wrists cupped or cocked, or whether he should swing flat or upright. He has learned the most important thing about golf swing without his mind being clouded with technicalities – that to hit golf shots well, the club has to be taken back reasonably straight and brought through reasonably straight, keeping the face of the club square to the intended line of flight.

As soon as he has learnt to do this with an 8 iron, he is ready to progress. He soon gets a mental picture of the shot and it's not long before he can do it with a slightly longer swing and with a 5 iron. The next step is to a lofted 3 wood, using exactly the same simple three-quarter swing, hitting the ball with very little effort and allowing the loft of the clubface to get the ball into the air. These shots should be played from a good lie, for at this stage the beginner needs all the help he can get, but it does give him the chance of hitting the ball. When he succeeds with a longer club, his confidence goes up by leaps and bounds.

When I first started teaching golf, I accepted what I had been taught by more experienced golf professionals. In those days we used to take weeks and weeks trying to teach a person the correct style and a sound swing, without ever letting him hit a golf ball. We reckoned that once he had fairly mastered the concepts of the swing and could produce it pretty well every time, he then had a reasonable chance of making contact with the ball nine times out of ten. Nowadays, people have far less time to waste. Not unnaturally they want to hit the ball almost from the outset because it is hitting the ball that gives them the encouragement they so badly need in the early days.

Many would-be golfers hit, or rather try to hit, the ball for the first time at a driving range without previously having any instruction from a qualified golf professional. Driving ranges have been responsible for introducing masses of people to this most wonderful of all sports, but unless a range is properly used it can be dangerous to a golfer's development. People with no previous experience step on to the range and, as it's a 'driving' range, they automatically take a driver. Because they've never had a lesson and barely know one end of the club from the other, they stand on the tee simply trying to knock the stuffing out of the sixty golf balls they've been given. They try to belt them as hard as they can, sometimes almost falling over in their attempts to make contact.

I've watched these folk on the driving range and I always feel so sorry that they've put the cart before the horse. They may hit one ball in the first ten attempts, so they'll try widening their stance a little, or bringing the feet close together, they'll take the club straight up on the backswing, or they'll swing it right round their waist, they'll try holding the club tightly, or they'll grip it loosely – all this in an attempt just to get the ball into the air and on its way down the range. It's all a waste of time if you have no idea of what you are trying to do and unless you have had one or two lessons to set you off on the right road. If these same embryo golfers started by trying to swing short clubs, learned a sound orthodox grip, easy footwork and developed the simple three-quarter swing that I recommended, quite soon they would be able to take their drivers out of the bag and hit the ball quite well with it.

At most driving ranges these days there is a resident professional staff to give lessons and make sure that the new golfer starts out on the right path. The driving range is also a most useful practice area, but it is of no use to anyone unless they know what they are practising and that a qualified teacher is there to see that pupils are practising the right things.

I have tried to explain in this chapter that the first lesson for a new golfer is probably the most important lesson in his golfing life. I don't think that anybody has the natural talent to pick up a golf club and start playing to a reasonable standard right from the word go, without any instruction. If you are keen to take up golf, start by having two or three lessons and concentrate on learning the correct grip, simple footwork, and good position at the top of the backswing, and a good finish.

Remember, too, that you won't hit the ball consistently until you have learned good balance and unless you watch the ball closely with the head reasonably still. It isn't necessary to keep your head completely immobile throughout the swing, as so many beginners believe, but it is as well not to have too much head movement, and absolutely vital that you don't take your eye off the ball.

You must work on keeping the swing moving smoothly back and forth, and always remember that it is a swinging action, not a hitting action. If you follow these rules, I'm sure that quite soon you'll be hitting the ball fairly consistently and you'll start to feel quite pleased with yourself. Once you start getting pleasure from it, you will have the incentive to come back to the golf course or to the driving range tomorrow or the next day, and you will be keen to rush home from work for a little practice in the garden. A true golfer will have been born.

Any good professional knows that he must keep these early lessons simple and easy for you to follow. He wants to give you the pleasure of hitting a golf ball just as quickly as he can, but he knows that you won't be able to do it if he has given you a hundred and one things to think about while you are trying to swing the club. That will only make you despondent about your progress. He is trained to do a skilled job, just as the architect who designed your house was a highly trained man. Would you think of completely designing your own house with all the technicalities involved? Then surely you wouldn't dream of developing a golf swing that has to last you the rest of your life without seeking expert advice. As time goes on and you realize that you have a firm grasp of the basics of the golf swing, then perhaps you will appreciate what a sound investment those first golf lessons were.

GRIP AND HAND ACTION

The first thing that the novice golfer has to master is the correct grip. We must never forget that, whatever the other actions of the golf swing, our hands are the only parts of the body that have contact with a golf club and their influence is responsible for the flight of the ball. A golfer is only as good as his hands: generally, the stronger the hands, the better the golfer will be.

It is the way that we place our hands on the golf club that determines whether we hit the ball straight, whether we hit it with a slight draw from right to left, or whether we hit it with fade from left to right.

There are three basic grips, of which the most popular and widely used is the overlapping or Vardon grip, so called because the great Harry Vardon was the first top professional to use it towards the end of the nineteenth century. With the overlapping grip, the little finger of the right hand rests in the niche between the index and second fingers of the left hand.

The interlocking grip is very similar, but the little finger of the right hand interlocks with the index finger of the left rather than resting on top of it. This grip is used by the world's No. 1 golfer Jack Nicklaus because he says it helps him to feel that both hands are working as one complete unit.

The third grip is the double-handed or baseball grip, where the hands are placed close together on the shaft, but the little finger of the right hand neither overlaps nor interlocks with the index finger of the left. This is often used by golfers who are not particularly strong because it permits greater power from the right hand. Dai Rees, who over many years has had a wonderful career as a professional, uses this grip in order to make up for his small stature. He finds that it helps him to keep up with the big boys.

For the sake of simplicity, I shall only describe the overlapping grip as this is widely accepted as being the orthodox hold on the club. If you want to experiment with the other grips, remember that they are exactly the same as the overlapping except for the relationship between the little finger of the right hand and the index finger of the left. All the other principles of gripping the club remain true.

First place your left hand on the shaft so that the grip of the club lies across the hand from the base of the little finger to the middle joint of the index finger. Now when you close the hand and wrap it round the grip you will see that a V has been formed between the index finger and the thumb. This V should be pointing midway between the chin and the right shoulder. Because the club has been angled slightly across the hand, you should feel that you are holding the club mainly with the fingers, but with a little assistance from the palm. If you feel that you are gripping with the palm, check your placing of the hand carefully.

Now wrap the fingers of the right hand round the shaft so that the little finger fits neatly into the groove *between* the index and second fingers, or *on* to the index finger, of the left hand. Once again you will notice a V formed between the thumb and index finger and, once again, the V should be aiming at a point between the chin and the right shoulder.

The index finger of the right hand should be crooked behind the shaft – almost as though you were about to squeeze the trigger on a gun.

Be careful to keep both the fingers and the hands close together. Although golf can never be anything but a two-handed game, the object of a good firm grip is to make the hands feel as much as possible like one single unit.

You should feel that the second, third and little fingers of the left hand and the two middle fingers of the right have firm control over the club and, while the grip should not be tight and cause you to tense up your hands and forearms, it must be firm enough not to allow the club to turn or twist in the hands at any point of the swing.

Many beginners, and even more experienced golfers, hold the club so near the end of the shaft that they don't really have a complete grip on it with the left hand. There should be an inch of shaft showing at the top once you've taken your grip. You will then be able to hold it firmly and also have more control over the clubface.

This grip will feel odd at first, simply because it is not the natural way to pick up a golf club. But every learner should make the effort to master this orthodox grip, and it's worth while practising it until it becomes almost second nature. Why not keep a club beside your chair while you're watching television? With this sort of practice it will soon begin to feel quite natural.

I cannot stress too much the importance of the grip; it is the basis of your whole golf game. Even though it is the most fundamental factor, it always amazes me how many poor grips there are in every golf club. Rarely do I see more than one or two members with sound orthodox grips – and until they learn that, they have no hope of hitting consistently good golf shots.

As we progress, we shall see that the key to good golf lies in strong hands and a good wrist action. Henry Cotton, perhaps the greatest of all British professionals, has always maintained that 'a golfer is only as good as his hands', and I think there's a lot of truth in that. That doesn't mean that people with small hands will never be able to play golf – indeed, small hands can be made very powerful. I think the best thing for improving the strength of your hands is golf itself and a lot of practice swinging, even if for only a few minutes each day, is bound to help tremendously.

If one were to study closely the actions of the first-class

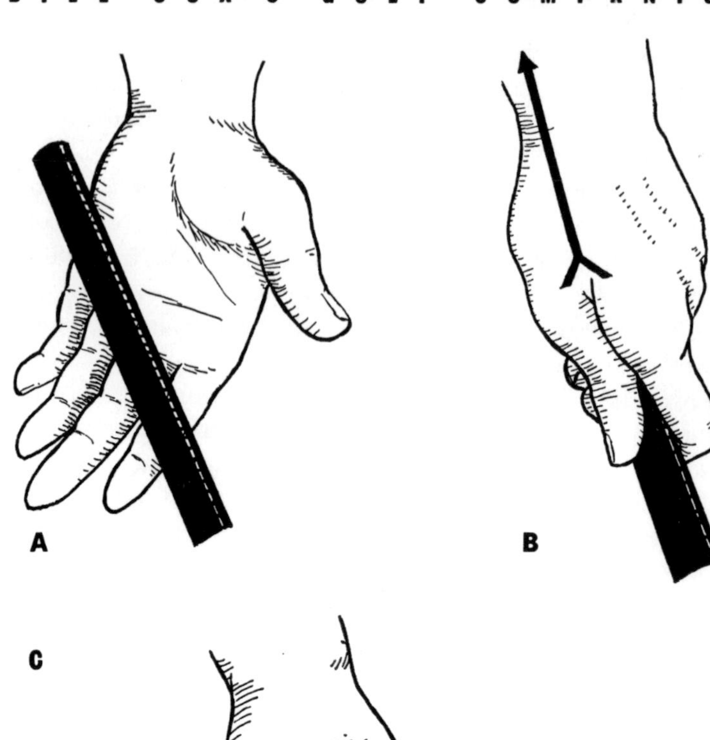

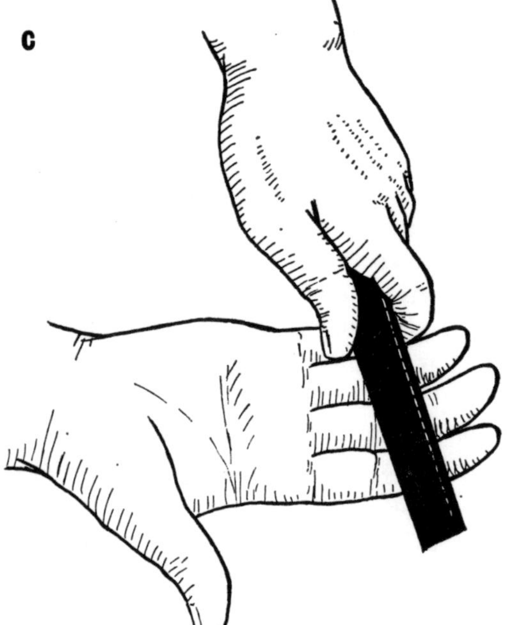

FIG. 1

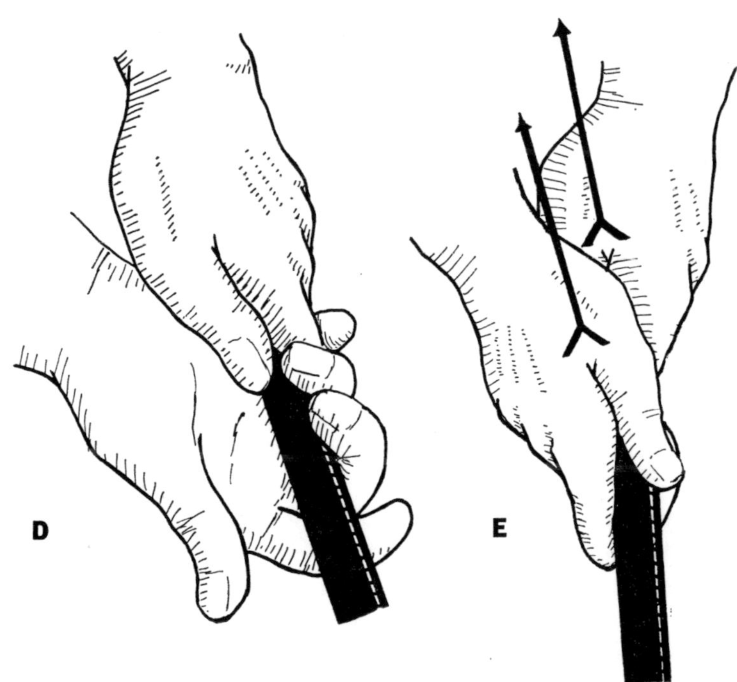

A. Shaft should be laid across left hand from base of little finger to middle joint of index finger.

B. When left hand closed, 'V' formed between index finger and thumb should point midway between chin and right shoulder.

C. Little finger of right hand overlaps index finger of left. Club is gripped basically with fingers—not palm.

D. Right hand then closed over left and over grip so that two hands feel like one unit.

E. Correct grip position with both 'Vs' parallel and pointing midway between chin and right shoulder. Right index finger 'triggered' to produce control and power.

professionals, one could not fail to notice that there is really a tremendous variation in their styles and movement. Some professionals have flat swings, others are more upright, some have long swings, others short, and so on. Nevertheless, through their hands all these players are able to feel exactly where the clubface is pointing at any part of the swing and, most important of all, at the moment of impact they know that the clubface is square to the ball and to the intended line of flight. These fellows' hands and wrists are in complete control of the clubhead all the time.

Generally speaking the swings of many average golfers compare quite favourably with these class players but, as I frequently tell my pupils, it is no good at all having a 6 handicap swing with a 26, or even 36, handicap hand action. So many players do not seem to realize just how bad their hand actions are. The majority of people do not control the clubhead or the shot at all with their hands – to them the hands are simply the means by which they swing the club back and swing it down.

The modern method of coaching is for the beginner to be shown the correct grip and hand action in the first few lessons. He is shown that, by slight variations of the position of the hands on the club, different types of shot can be produced. At this stage it is not important, indeed it could be confusing, to learn how to hook the ball, or how to slice it, by slightly shifting the position of the hands, but by demonstrating this the professional teacher can make his pupil understand just how important it is to have the hands correctly placed at the outset of the swing. If you don't take up the correct grip, it means that you will have to try to manipulate the clubface during the swing itself. This could throw the swing completely out of gear and out of its groove, and it is certainly a very dangerous thing for the weekend golfer to attempt He is bound to hit erratic shots.

Whatever style you may develop, whether you play with an open, shut or square clubface at the top of the backswing, you must at all times be able to control the clubface so that at the moment of impact it is square to the back of the ball. And I think it is important to concentrate on this thoughout your swing. You will not come squarely into the ball unless you *make* yourself square. It's amazing how, if you 'think square', the brain tells the hands what to do and makes them feel aware of their position in relation to the clubface.

For most golfers, the 'strong' position for the left hand is important in the grip. This simply means that when you look down at your hands on the club, you should be able to see either two, or two and a half, knuckles of the left hand. This will mean that the left hand V will be pointing about midway between the chin and right shoulder, and the V of the right hand will be pointing in exactly the same spot. With this grip, as long as the wrists do not roll the clubface open or twist it shut on the backswing, you should be able to achieve a square clubface position at the top of the backswing.

Most beginners are plagued with a slice or cut, when the ball veers sharply to the right. It is the beginner's commonest complaint. There could be many reasons for it, but as often as not, the cause of the trouble lies in the grip. For these people the strong left-hand position is absolutely essential, and if they want to hit the ball dead straight, or even with a little draw, they should concentrate hard on not allowing the clubface to roll open on the backswing.

Many golfers do not achieve maximum clubhead speed at impact, and therefore maximum distance, because they have not learnt to cock their wrists well – they are not fully cocked at the top of the backswing. If you're guilty of this fault, you can soon prove to yourself just how important a full wrist-cock is to the golf swing. Try hitting some 5-iron shots with no wrist action at all. Take your hands as high as the right shoulder without cocking the wrists and try hitting the ball hard simply with your arms. You'll do well if you reach fifty yards. Now try a few shots using a very short swing, but with the wrists fully

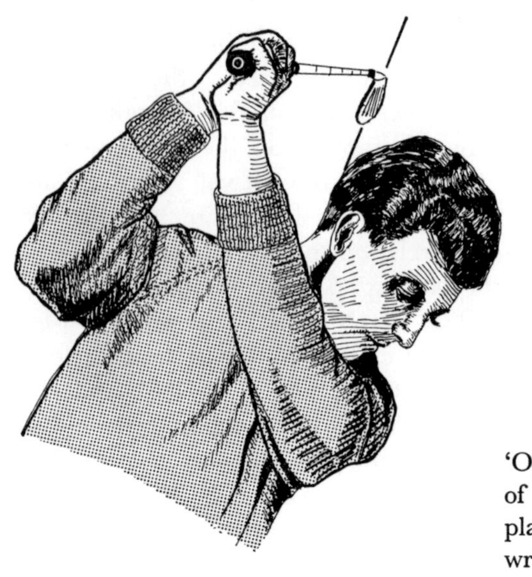

FIG. 2

'Open' position at top of backswing where player has cupped left wrist at top of swing.

FIG. 3

Player has twisted left hand and forearm so that clubface is in 'shut' position at top of swing.

FIG. 4
If no rolling of hands and arms during backswing, orthodox grip should produce 'square' clubface position at top of swing.

cocked at shoulder height. Use maximum wrist action as you come into the impact area, and you'll be surprised how much distance you can get with this simple yet powerful wrist-action shot.

Having established the fact that it is the hands and wrists that must control the shot throughout, the next step is to strengthen and develop them. Any exercise involving the hands is good: the South African wizard, Gary Player, is a great believer in fingertip press-ups, although that sort of thing is beyond most of us unless we are very young and keen. I'm a great believer in 'golf for golf'. By that I mean that if you want to develop a good golf swing, there is no better way than practising the swing and, if you want to develop good strong hands, what better way is there than making them do the job you are developing them to do? Plenty of practice swinging will not only develop your hand action; it will be developing all the other parts of the swing at the same time.

One of the greatest lessons in golf came from Jack Nicklaus, just after he had won the Open Championship at Muirfield in 1966, when he said: 'I knew exactly what I was doing with the ball. I could feel every shot through my hands and wrists.' It was a feeling that won Jack the Open, but it also is the feeling that every other golfer should strive for. When you've got it, you've found the secret of golf.

STANCE AND LEG ACTION

The experienced teacher or golf watcher can recognize a good player even before he swings and hits the ball. I weigh up a player by two things initially: the way he grips the club and the way he shapes up to the ball.

If you've concentrated on learning a good, sound grip, you've gone a long way to learning golf, but obviously a good grip and hand action are no use at all unless you have set yourself up in such a way that you can use your hands to their best advantage. If you are going to hit the ball at all well, you must put yourself in a position to hit it.

It will be clear to you by now that I am a great believer in orthodoxy, so I recommend the 'square' stance – that is to say, with the feet at an angle of ninety degrees to the intended line of flight. An *open* stance is where the *left* foot is slightly drawn back from this line, when one wants to produce a faded shot. A *closed* stance is where the *right* foot is drawn slightly back, when one wants to produce draw. You may eventually find that one of these stances suits your game better, but for the time being I suggest you concentrate on setting yourself up squarely.

For full shots, the feet should be placed as far apart as the width of the player's shoulders, or just a fraction wider, with the toes pointing slightly outwards. You will find that this width is best for helping you to retain your balance throughout the swing.

Of course, there are exceptions to practically every rule in golf, but usually these exceptions among good players are developed over years of experience to suit the individual. That very good American professional, Doug Sanders, straddles his

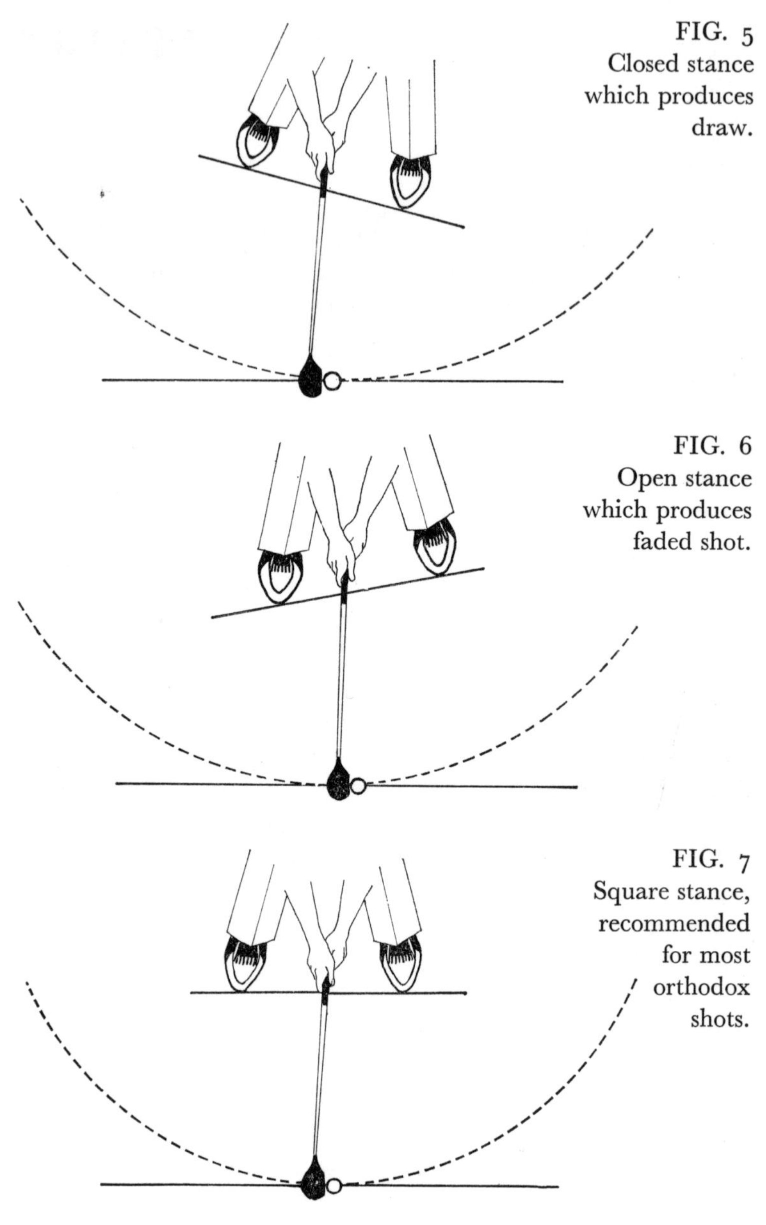

FIG. 5
Closed stance which produces draw.

FIG. 6
Open stance which produces faded shot.

FIG. 7
Square stance, recommended for most orthodox shots.

feet very wide apart at the address position, and then hits the ball with an ultra-short swing. It looks rather strange, but Doug plays very well with this method. If, however, he used a full-length swing, he would find that he could not turn at all well from his wide stance.

You will never hit the ball well unless you feel comfortable and relaxed, so the knees should be slightly bent and there must be no tension at all in the legs. This will give you far greater freedom in the pivot than if the legs are kept straight and stiff. Your weight should be evenly distributed between your toes and heels, both at address and throughout the swing. It is absolutely fatal to allow the weight to rock too much either on to the toes or on to the heels.

A tremendous number of players make the mistake of leaning too much weight on the left foot at address by bending the left knee too much and keeping the right leg straight. This is likely to cause a steep backswing and a sort of 'chopping' action. Others have the same fault in reverse. They straighten the left leg, bend the right knee, and have all their weight on the right leg. This means that they are almost completely locked before they even start the backswing.

It is important, then, to find a balance between the two extremes and that both legs should 'look' the same to you before you address the ball. You should be slightly knock-kneed, with both knees turned very slightly in towards the ball as you take up your stance but be careful not to overdo this. If the left knee is pointing in too much, it is likely to encourage a swing round the body, a very flat action. On the other hand, the knees should never be pointing outwards. This will only lock the hip action and impede a good hip pivot.

All good golfers develop a 'drill' for getting into the correct address position, so that even when they are playing in the crucial stages of a tournament and they are under terrific pressure, habit ensures that they will be standing properly to the ball.

FIG. 8

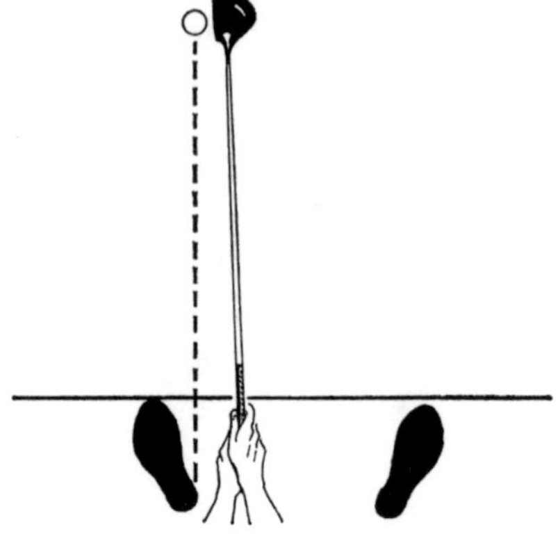

A. Driver address position.

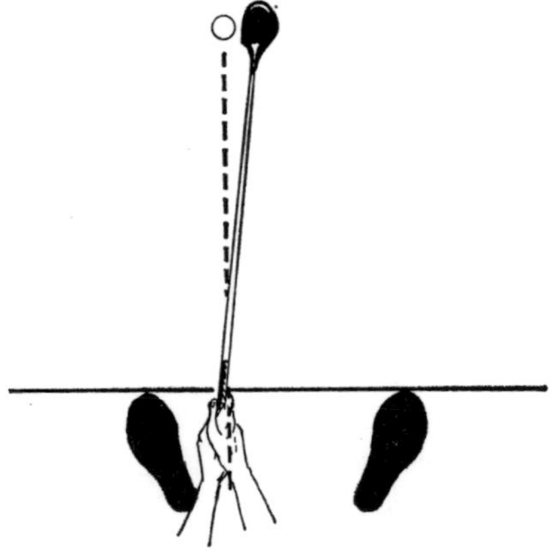

B. Fairway wood address position – same position used for long irons.

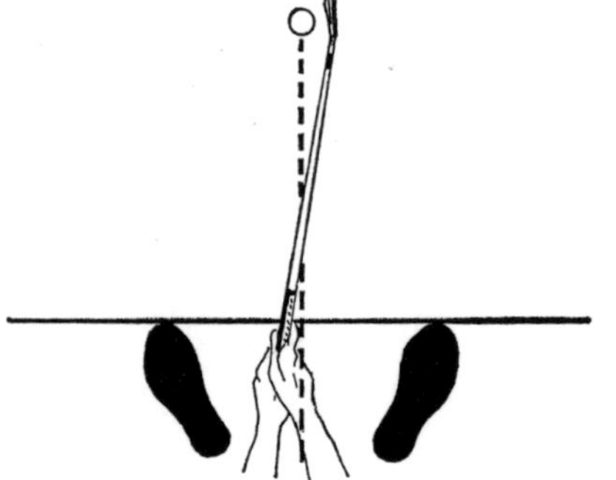

C. Mid-iron address position – used with nos. 4, 5, 6 and 7 irons.

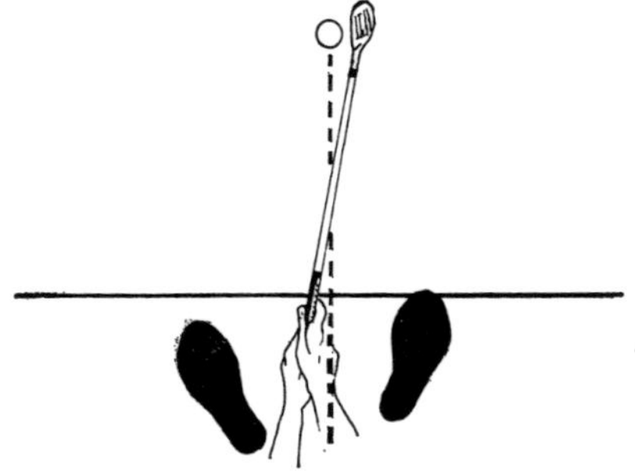

D. Slightly open stance with hands in advance of club-head for lofted pitch shot.

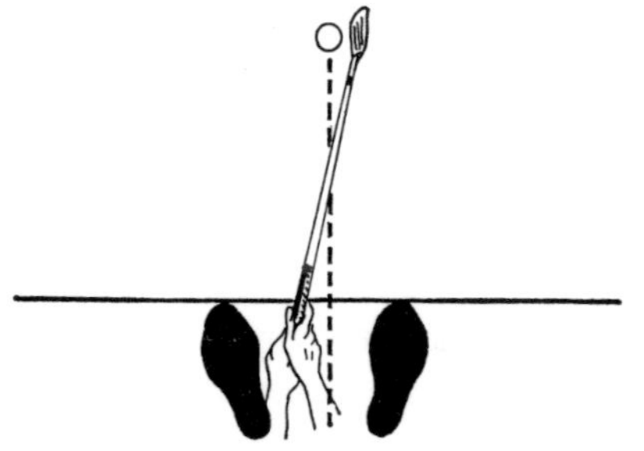

E. Narrow square stance with hands advanced for chip shot.

This is the drill I recommend: first tee the ball up (if you are playing from the tee, of course!) and then stand about six feet behind it so that you are looking directly down the fairway at the target. Take up your correct grip; you might have a little waggle, or a short practice swing, just to make sure that the grip is firm and to limber up the wrist action. Keep looking at your point of aim, and try to build up a mental picture of the sort of shot you are going to play. Even try to imagine how high you are going to play the shot – it's amazing how big a part auto-suggestion plays in golf.

Now you are ready to move round to the side of the ball.

Place the clubhead about an inch behind the ball, making absolutely sure that the clubface is at exact right angles to your line of flight, and that you are addressing the ball right in the centre of the face – not off the toe or the heel of the club.

As you put the clubhead down behind the ball, place your right foot in its correct position. Then put the left foot in place remembering that a line through your toes should be exactly parallel with the line of flight. If you were to draw a line through your shoulders and through your hips, you would find that these, too, are parallel.

If you have your knees properly flexed, you should look as though you are just about to sit down in a chair. But be careful not to crouch down too much; keep your back reasonably straight and you will be standing in a good position. The important thing is that you should feel comfortable and relaxed – able to swing back and through the ball without losing balance. The hands and arms and club should all feel like one unit – and they should look it, too, for they should be in more or less a straight line, with the hands just a fraction in front of the clubhead.

This, then, is the address position for a long shot, but the principles remain exactly the same for all other shots, the only difference being that, on short iron strokes, the feet can be placed quite close together and in a slightly open position. This means that you will take the club back a little more steeply, which in turn will produce a higher-flying shot.

Wooden clubs do not have very much loft on the face, so, to help you get the ball into the air, you place the ball well forward in your stance – about an inch inside the left heel for a driver or a number 2 wood, an inch further back for the 3 and 4 woods, yet another inch back for the shallow-faced long irons – the 2, 3 and 4. Practically all the other clubs can be played from the centre of the feet for the sake of simplicity, but it is *absolutely imperative* that you do not play any golf shot from further back than centre of the feet.

With this address position, your feet should feel 'alive' and your legs ready to respond. They have an important job to do, for it is the feet and legs that help to give you that extra bit of power.

On the backswing, the weight that has been evenly distributed on both feet moves back almost totally on to the right foot, with the left knee breaking inwards slightly to point behind the ball and the left heel rising from the ground. How far the left heel rises varies considerably. Some top players raise it as much as two inches, others barely at all. The beginner should be warned against lifting it too high.

One of the most important changes in leg action since the last war is the position of the right knee at the top of the swing. In my youth it was considered vital to straighten and push back with the right leg as soon as possible on the backswing so that it was absolutely straight and stiff. Nowadays this is considered absolutely wrong and from watching the top American golfers we have learnt that the best technique is to keep the right knee as flexed at the top of the backswing as it was at the address position.

During the downswing, too, both knees remain flexed and turn slightly so that they are almost aiming along the line of flight. As you come into the downswing you add yet more power to the hands by thrusting through with the right leg – it's a combination of a push with the inside of the right shoe and a 'kick' with the knee.

For many years Britain's golf professionals stressed the importance of bracing the whole of the left side either at, or just before, the moment of impact. Once again, this is an area of the golf swing where we have learnt the error of our ways, because this braced left-side method simply blocks the swing, restricts the follow-through, and prevents the player from getting full power into the shot. It used to be widely taught and many people tried to do it; nowadays we know better, and no good player tries to keep the left side braced. Let your full weight go through on a flexed left knee and allow the hands and body to go through to a stylish follow-through.

Only two parts of the body have any contact with an outside agency – the hands on the club and the feet on the ground. It is from these two parts of the anatomy that the golfer derives nearly all his power. The hands whip into the ball, and the feet pour all the other power resources into the shot through the legs. If he is to use this power, a player must be standing correctly and comfortably to the ball and it is worth the time checking and double-checking on the practice ground to make sure that you are setting yourself up properly. As with the grip, it is one of those basics of golf where you can so easily slip into bad habits without noticing. Then when you hit bad shots you start looking for faults in the swing, rather than trying to find what might be a relatively simple fault in your set-up position.

THE SWING: ARM AND SHOULDER ACTION

Have you noticed how when you are watching experts doing anything, they manage to make it look incredibly easy? Juggling acts on television are always impressive, for although the performers do all sorts of complex tricks, everything is apparently done so slowly and deliberately and they rarely make a mistake. Practice, of course, makes perfect, but there is more to it than that. They are combining technical prowess with balance and rhythm.

The golf swing is much the same, and balance and rhythm play a tremendous part in it, too. I shall have more to say about this later but what I want to impress upon you at this point is that the golf swing is complete in itself, an apparently unhurried, free-flowing movement. For this reason, I am not breaking the backswing, downswing and follow-through into different sections. You must not think of them as being different parts of the swing, otherwise you will end up with a jerky action which is not a complete entity.

The hands actually hit the ball, or direct the clubface into the back of the ball, the feet and legs make sure that the rest of the body is in a good position to hit the ball, but it is the arms that makes the golf action a complete and smooth thing. Golf is a two-handed game, so it must be a game where both arms are used fully in order to get the correct movement and to get maximum power into the shot.

The left arm and hand predominate on the backswing. They almost push the club to the top of the swing. The first movement must be one piece – by that I mean that the left hand, arm, left knee, shoulder and the clubhead all move back as one complete unit. The hands do not pick up the clubhead by breaking the wrists quickly on the backswing. The wrists must stay firm. You should feel that the left shoulder is pushing the arms up as it turns.

At about waist height it is natural for the wrists to start cocking – there is no need to make any conscious effort to do

FIG. 9

A. Takeaway swing is 'one-piece' movement with hands, arms and shoulders moving back as complete unit.

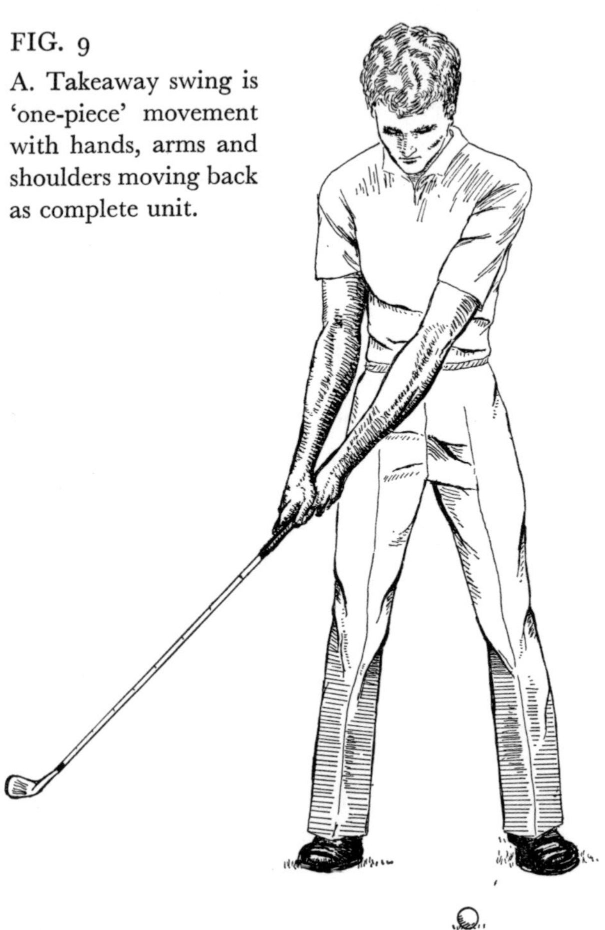

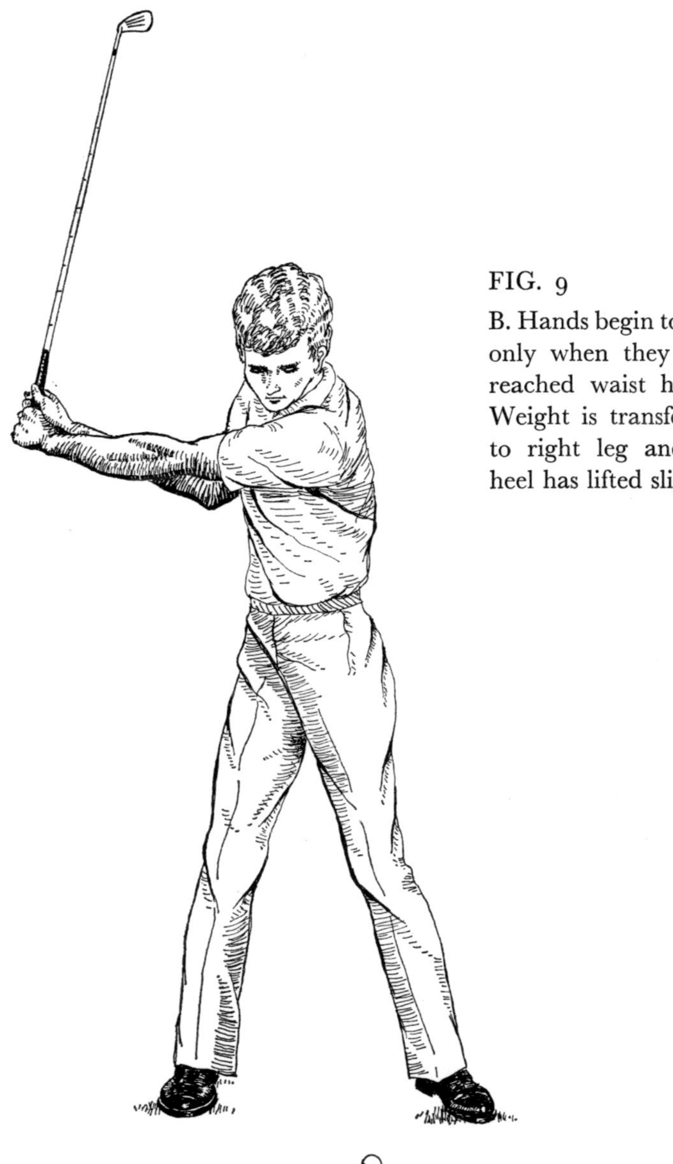

FIG. 9

B. Hands begin to cock only when they have reached waist height. Weight is transferring to right leg and left heel has lifted slightly.

this – but the left arm must remain quite straight, acting rather like the spoke of a wheel. As the left arm remains straight, the right arm tucks underneath with the elbow pointing to the ground.

FIG. 9

C. At top of swing practically all weight is on right leg and there has been full shoulder turn. Left arm is kept as straight as possible with hands fully in control of club.

The first arm movement of the downswing is that the right elbow returns close to the side, with the wrists fully cocked. You are now on an inside groove and in a position to hit the ball squarely.

FIG. 9

D. Lateral hip slide, moving weight to left, initiates downswing. Legs flexed and relaxed; right elbow quickly returns to side and hands remain fully cocked.

With the left arm still straight and pulling the clubhead down towards the ball, the right hand whips into the shot at the moment of impact, with the hands travelling on towards the target. At the exact point of contact, you should be in exactly the same position as you were at address, but with the weight

FIG. 9

E. As hips slide forward, they also turn to left, allowing player to hit on inside-to-out plane.

on the left foot, the right heel off the ground and the right knee pointing at the ball.

On the follow-through, the right shoulder passes under the chin as the hands and arms swing through the ball. Although you have hit the shot with both hands, it is now the right hand

FIG. 9

F. At last possible moment hands accelerate clubhead squarely into back of ball. Right leg 'kicks' into shot with all weight now on left foot.

and arm that predominate, for the left arm folds so that the elbow is pointing to the ground and the hands go on into a high, stylish follow-through.

One of the most important things in the arm action is to have the left arm as straight as is possible with comfort on the back-swing. This will give you a consistent width to the arc of your swing and this will mean fewer topped shots and less 'digging'

FIG. 9

G. Although ball now on its way, player still watches spot from where ball has just been hit.

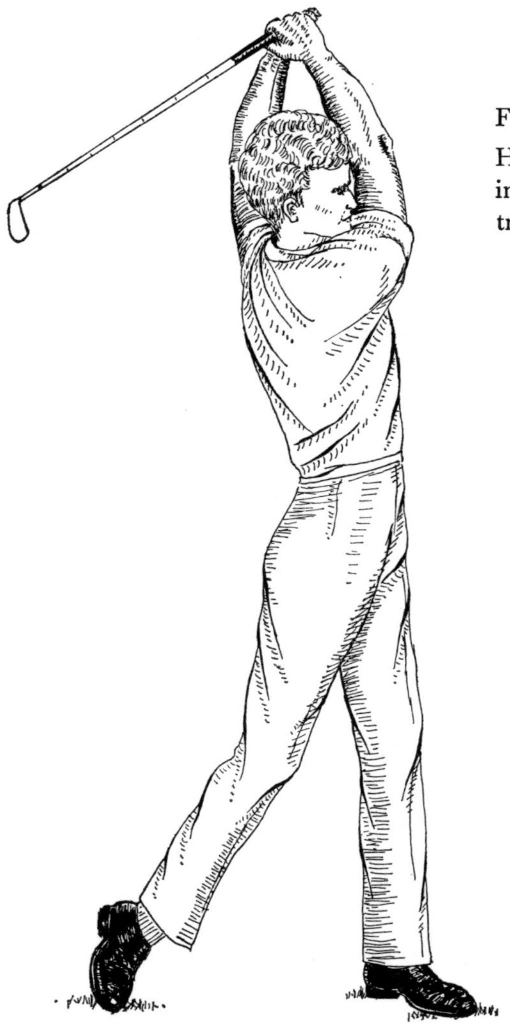

FIG. 9

H. Hands finish high in attractive and controlled follow-through.

for the ball. There are still a few first-class players who do not have their left arms absolutely straight on the backswing, but in most cases the bend is only very slight, and they come into the ball with it very nearly straight and always in a good position. From my experience with pupils who come to me with a bent left arm, I find that when they first try to straighten it, they stiffen it too much. But after one or two practice sessions, this stiffness soon disappears and the swing starts to look very much better and to give more consistent results.

The other vital thing is to make sure that the right arm is close to the side when you start the downswing. If it doesn't get into position very quickly you are going to hit some very wild shots, for you are almost certain to swing across the ball from outside-to-in, which will impart a slicing spin.

All club golfers get a thrill out of knocking the ball a long way, and many ruin their games in an effort to do just this. Yet there are still far too many weekend golfers who seem to be afraid of using their strong right arms. They seem to think that the right hand and arm should only be used at the very last moment before striking the ball. But if one is to achieve maximum power *both* hands and *both* arms must be used fully throughout the swing.

Remember too that the golf swing doesn't finish at impact. As you follow through, keep that right arm travelling straight at the target for as long as you can. It will help to control the shot and give it a little more power.

One of the commonest faults that affect low-handicap golfers almost as much as beginners and long handicappers is using too much shoulder action to start the downswing. In other words, instead of the right shoulder coming down, under the chin and through, it comes out, round the chin and over. This immediately throws the clubhead on an outside groove, and if the clubface is open the shot will be badly sliced, or if the clubface is closed, the ball will be pulled well to the left of the target.

I find that players with weak or untrained hands are the ones most likely to develop this fault because they subconsciously use their strong shoulder muscles at the start of the downswing in order to compensate for their weak hands.

A good cure for shoulder 'roll' is to keep the left arm perfectly straight and the left shoulder up at the address position. Take the club back slightly on the inside groove with the shoulders turning fully and the legs relaxed. By a full shoulder turn I mean that the shoulders should turn through a full ninety degrees between the address and top of the backswing position. How much the left shoulder dips down on the backswing depends on the club you use – the shorter the club, the greater the tilt. If you are using a driver and you want to hit a long one with draw which gives it topspin, then try to keep your left shoulder quite well up on the backswing.

At the start of the downswing you must transfer your weight to the left foot and make a conscious effort to keep the shoulders wound up until the arms have brought the clubhead into the hitting area. Only then can you let fly with your whole body, including the shoulders, and try to bring that clubface fast and square into the back of the ball.

Plenty of practice swings are the only way to get the arms and shoulders working together and the only way to give your shots more power, but it is only if you remember that everything must follow the hands that you will start to improve. Once the arms, shoulders, or any other part of the body start taking control of the hands, there is no way you can hit good golf shots consistently.

THE HEAD AND HIP ACTION

Without any doubt, the head is blamed for more bad shots than any other part of the body, and 'head-up' is probably still the most common fault that golfers make nearly every time they play. Since time immemorial, beginners have been advised to 'keep the head down', but personally I think this is very bad advice because, if you take it at face value, it can lead to all sorts of errors. I see a lot of players who, in an effort to keep their heads 'down', literally force their chins hard down on their chests. This, of course, restricts the backswing, as all these players succeed in doing is picking the clubhead up too steeply, almost like a meat cleaver, and then stabbing down on to the ball with practically no follow-through.

I am not a believer in keeping the head down nor in keeping it absolutely still – although I think it is bad to move it too much during the swing. The best advice I can give is to 'watch the ball closely' rather then to keep the head *down*. Many first-class players do move their heads slightly during the swing – indeed, it is very difficult, if not almost impossible, to keep it dead still – but in all cases where it is a noticeable movement, these players are known as good watchers of the ball. This more than compensates for any slight movement.

Another bad fault is pushing the head down towards the ball during the backswing – a sort of dipping action. Again, this is quite often caused by heeding the advice 'keep your head down'. You can usually spot this fault either on a long shot, like a drive, or on a short pitch. The player is desperately afraid of moving his head with the big drive swing; with the pitch because there is little body movement, he gets tensed up, but is determined to keep his head still. In either case the result is the same – the club is taken back far to steeply, and with a chopping action the shot is fluffed, hitting the ground behind the ball.

Although there is no objection to a little lateral movement of the head (although it's unwise to have too much of it), beware of allowing the head to dip down or to lift upwards, which is bound to cause a topped shot.

Another piece of advice that is often given to beginners is to tilt the head and chin slightly backwards, so that you are only looking at the ball with the left eye. The reason this is recommended by some teachers is so that the chin will not interfere with the left shoulder on the backswing. I can't agree with this tip because, if you are going to be a good watcher of the ball, I think you've got to watch it with both eyes.

In teaching I don't concentrate too much on hip action – in fact, to do so is bound to put anybody off their game. If you think too much about hips, you are almost bound to forget about your hands – and it is in the hands that the secret of good golf lies. Nevertheless, it is important for the new golfer to understand the importance of the hips in the golf swing, although he will find that if he carries out the correct leg and foot actions, the hips will function properly without his even having to think about it.

Interest was focused on hip action when the great American professional, Ben Hogan, surely one of the most accurate strikers of all time, attributed much of his power to the fast unwinding and lateral movement of his left hip during the downswing. He considered that this action helped him to create much greater clubhead speed at the moment of impact. Suddenly this was accepted into the modern method of teaching, but I wonder whether those who accepted it appreciated just how dangerous this movement could be. Hogan was successful with it because he was an exceptionally talented man and also because he was in a position to hit hundreds of golf shots every day whereas, for the average player, unwinding the hips too early can cause the right shoulder to unwind as well, throwing the clubhead on the outside groove and producing the bad fault of coming across the ball. It really is quite difficult to unwind the hips without unwinding the shoulders at the same time.

I think that on the backswing there should be a combination of hip pivot and lateral movement which slides the weight across to favour the right foot at the top of the backswing. At the top the hips should have turned through about forty-five degrees. But on the downswing you are courting disaster if you think in terms of unwinding the hips: you would be much nearer the mark if you thought simply of sliding the hips into the shot. (See Figs. 9d and e, pp. 117–18.)

What actually happens is that the hips move laterally and transfer the weight to the left foot at the same time as they are turning of their own accord. To get maximum clubhead speed and power they must move fairly quickly – a sluggish hip action never produces a long ball. I must stress again that it is a fast hip *slide*, not a fast hip *unwind*.

This method of using the hips also helps a player to keep the clubface square for a longer period in the impact area without losing either balance or clubhead speed. It helps to create that attractive long, wide follow-through. To help the hips do their job, don't brace the left knee as you are coming into the ball; let it 'give' a little so that the whole of the lower part of your body is sliding foward while the head remains steady.

Good hip action will help you to hit the ball farther and also straighter because the face of the club is square to the line of flight longer. But the beginner really needn't worry about making the hips do their job; as long as his leg and arm actions are right, the hips will go about their business.

The hip slide only became fashionable after golf teachers had stopped trying to make their pupils keep a braced left side. Obviously, with a rigid right leg at the top of the backswing and a rigid left leg at impact, it was not possible to slide the hips; only to turn them. Once we accepted that the legs should be thoroughly relaxed and flexed throughout the entire swing, it became quite natural for the hips to slide laterally. Thus the modern hip action is an effect, not a cause.

It all comes back, then, to the legs and the hands. Strong legs are a tremendous asset to the golfer. If he has powerful legs, he can get that much more thrust into the back of the ball. I well remember a man coming to me for a lesson, and although he had only about a twelve handicap he hit the ball as far as any amateur I've ever seen, and as far as most top professionals. I was fascinated by the speed of his leg action, which in turn gave him a very quick hip action. It was then he told me that in his youth he had won the 440 yards for Scotland, and he still had terrifically powerful legs.

My advice to the beginner regarding hip action is simply this: learn and appreciate the task that the hips have to perform – and then forget about them. It's as simple as that.

THROUGH THE BAG

The drive is probably the most important stroke on every hole. It sets you up to make your figures, and gives you a tremendous psychological boost if you feel confident of your ability to hit the ball consistently about two hundred yards down the middle. If most club golfers could do that, they would automatically halve their handicaps because the second shots would be made so much more easy. It's all very well quoting the old saying: 'You drive for show, but putt for dough,' but if your drive doesn't put you in a good spot and you are always having to hack out of the rough, not even the greatest putter in the business can consistently return good scores.

THE DRIVER

The driver is the least lofted of the wooden clubs, so naturally it flights the ball lower through the air and for a longer distance than, say, an 8 iron. There are many drivers on the market these days that are too straight-faced and this makes it difficult for the beginner to get the ball into the air at all. Most club golfers would be well advised to look for a driver that has ten or twelve degrees of loft – you won't find many professionals using a driver with much less loft than that. For beginners it is not a bad plan to drive with a brassie, or number 2 wood. This has a slightly shallower face and a little more loft, and this automatically gives the player confidence in his ability to get the ball into the air without trying to 'scoop' it up. You won't find that you lose much in the way of length – only a yard or two – and this is more than compensated by being able to hit the ball consistently into the air and down the fairway.

Many beginners seem to believe that the heavier the club, the farther you will hit the ball. This is far from true, for if the club is too heavy for you, it is not possible to control it properly and there is bound to be a loss in power. There is a trend nowadays towards lighter clubs, and the longest driver in the world, Jack Nicklaus, uses a club that feels almost like a toothpick when you pick it up.

Perhaps the address position plays a greater part in the long shots than in any other department of the game. When using a driver or brassie from the tee, it is important to keep the hands up, so that there is a very slight arch in the wrists, and also to keep the hands fractionally ahead of the ball when you set yourself up. If you let your hands hang low and behind the ball, you are going to hit all manner of wild shots, but particularly you are going to hit the ball very high.

Position the ball an inch or so inside the left heel, so that you are hitting it forward and you will be able to get it airborne without any scooping action. The toes should be pointing slightly outwards to give you a firm base. You can then transfer your weight freely without any loss of balance.

The driver is the longest club in the bag, so if you are going to keep control over it throughout the shot, you must give the swing plenty of time and use a smooth action. Just because the club is designed to hit the ball a long way doesn't mean that you have to 'flash' at it. On the other hand, don't feel too restricted or afraid with this club. That sort of attitude will only lead to a guided shot with a short, poking swing. Feel free and relaxed, and swing the club smoothly without any inhibitions. If you stick to the swing principles I have already suggested, you will find that you can drive a good distance consistently straight. Don't be fooled into thinking that you have to try and drive as far as possible every time. This will lead to inconsistency and mistiming of the ball. There are some very good golfers around who don't hit their tee shots an almighty distance, but still score very well because they are hardly ever off the fairway.

THE FAIRWAY WOODS

The fairway woods are the numbers 2, 3 and 4, the 2 wood, or brassie, having the least loft, and the 4 wood the greatest. Generally, my advice to weekend golfers and beginners is to forget about using the brassie on the fairway. When the ball is teed up, it can give you great confidence, but it is very rare that you find a good enough fairway lie to use this relatively straight-faced club, and ninety-nine times out of a hundred the inexperienced golfer will only top the ball along the ground.

The swing does not vary on any of these long shots, only the address position, so if you find yourself with a wonderful lie on the fairway and you have a level stance and the pin is 200 yards away, position the ball just ahead of the centre point between the feet with the hands slightly ahead of the ball. However, the opportunities for using this club are rare, and it is far wiser for the long handicap player to think twice before playing it.

The 3 wood has a slightly shorter shaft and a little more loft than the 2 and, because it is a fairly simple club to use, it is the club golfer's constant friend.

A good 3 wood player can consistently hit greens that are out of range for the iron clubs, find the green at long par-three holes, and hit long shots from rather close lies.

With the driver the ball is hit very cleanly (there must be no hitting the turf either before or after the ball) but a 3 wood is played rather more like an iron. The ball must be struck a descending blow with a little turf taken after impact. It should be a punchy, compact swing. Where so many golfers go wrong is in trying to scoop the ball into the air with a 3 wood, and falling back on to the right foot.

When you're using a 3 wood, position the ball a couple of inches inside the left heel and try to get the feeling that you are hitting right down and through the ball. The generous loft on the face of the club will make sure that the shot soars through the air.

If you pull your right foot back slightly so the stance is a little closed, and play the ball from midway between the feet with the clubface slightly hooded on the backswing, you will produce a low boring shot that runs a long way when it touches down. As long as you haven't any bunkers to carry, this is a very effective stroke in the wind.

The 4 wood has even more loft and the sole of the club is well rounded so that the shallow face can get down into really 'cuppy' lies. It is played in exactly the same way as a number 3 wood, but the flight of the ball is rather higher. This makes it an ideal weapon if you have a longish shot – say, 180 yards – into a green that is well bunkered in front. It also means that it can go through semi rough, and even heather, quite successfully. No long-handicap golfer can afford to be without a 4 wood, and for the beginner this and a 2 wood for use on the tee make the ideal armoury of wooden clubs. Once again, make sure that you hit down on the ball with a punchy, late-hitting action. The 4 wood will not do its job properly if you try to help the ball into the air and fall back on your right leg in the attempt.

THE LONG IRONS

Nothing gives greater satisfaction, to my mind, than to hit a 2 or 3 iron sweetly off the middle of the clubface and watch it fly like a bullet at the flagstick, but these are clubs that the good golfer uses far more successfully than the beginner and the long-handicap player. They require a good sound swing as well as strength and flexibility in the player.

I am not suggesting that the beginner should leave the 2 and 3 irons in the bag and forget about them. By all means go to the practice ground and learn how to use them – it will certainly make you a more complete golfer, but I would suggest that, until you are quite proficient with them, you favour the 3 and 4 wood during an actual game on the course.

Most golfers are frightened by the long irons simply by looking at their design. They are shallow-headed clubs with little loft, and the inexperienced golfer's immediate reaction is: 'I'll never be able to get the ball up with *that.*' This subconsciously causes him to try and help the ball into the air by scooping and causes a lot of topped shots. As with the fairway woods, the important thing to remember about the long irons is that you must hit *down* on the ball – the loft is sufficient to get the ball up to the height you want it.

At address, have the ball about three inches inside the left heel and make sure that your fingers have a firm grip on the club. This is important because, after hitting the ball, you should take a little turf and it is all too easy for the head of a long iron to twist when it makes contact with the ground. It is vital that you carry out the 'ball/turf sequence' – that is, that you hit the ball first and because the clubhead is still travelling downwards, and then take a small divot after the ball.

The address position is much the same as for a fairway wood, making sure that the club and left arm are in a straight line. The smooth, one-piece takeaway should ensure that the clubface remains square and at the top of the swing the club should be pointing directly at the target.

I have tried to impress on you the importance of transferring the weight to the left foot at the start of the downswing on all shots, but nowhere is this movement more important than on a long iron shot, for this will more or less guarantee that you are hitting *down* on to the ball. For the same reason it is important to delay uncocking the wrists until the very last moment – the later you hit the ball the better; in fact, you should feel that your hands are ahead of the clubhead at the moment of impact.

Because they don't feel confident with these clubs, which have been designed to hit the ball a long way, many golfers seem to think that the only way to play long irons is to take

A

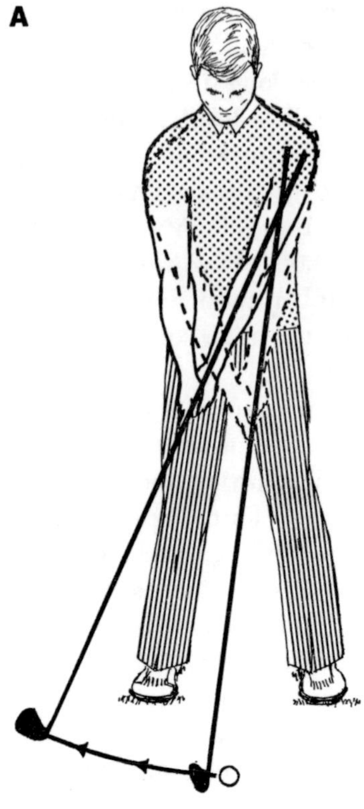

FIG. 10 A and B

On all shots takeaway should be one-piece (*see* A). Too many club golfers start backswing with quick wrist-break (*see* B); only time this is permissible is when player must get pitch shot into air quickly.

a vicious fast swipe at the ball. That will never produce good shots in a million years. Smoothness and rhythm are all important with these shots and players should let the length of the shaft produce the power they want rather than try to produce it with a desperate shoulder heave.

The long irons are wonderful clubs, particularly in a strong wind, where they keep the ball flying lower, and thus less likely to be blown off line, than the 3 or 4 wood. In spite of this, my advice to new golfers is to master the wooden clubs first because they are your stock-in-trade and you will be using a wooden club at least once on nearly every hole. The long irons

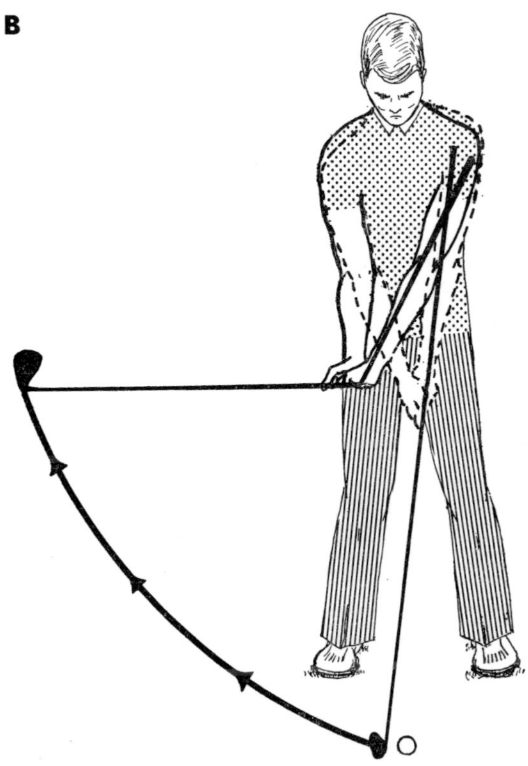

are much more difficult to play and you are likely to need them much less often. When you can hit your woods and mid-irons well, then by all means start concentrating on your long-iron shots.

THE MID-IRONS

The mid-irons, the numbers 4, 5 and 6, are probably the most important clubs in your bag. Wonderful driving is no use at all unless you can follow it up by putting the ball on to the green nine times out of ten. Most golfers get a kick out of seeing the ball soaring away from the tee after a good drive, or boring towards the flag after a crisply hit fairway wood, so these are often the shots that club players practise most – simply because they get pleasure from hitting them.

Not nearly enough time is spent on the dull old mid-irons, because, after all, you can't hit the ball far with them, can you? This is stupid thinking, of course, for it is invariably the shots from between 170 yards and 130 yards from the flag that either make or break your score. More often than not you will be using one of these clubs for your second shot at many par-four holes and, if you can consistently put the ball on the green, it means that you will have two putts for a par. If you can consistently put the ball on the green *and near the hole*, you are going to give yourself plenty of chances to make a single putt and score a birdie.

The mid-irons are not designed to hit the ball terrific distances but they are designed to be used with great accuracy; when you watch some of the world's best professionals using these clubs, you suddenly appreciate what it is that makes the professional so much better than the club golfer.

Because you are not trying to hit the ball hard but are trying to hit it straight, it is a good idea to restrict the length of your swing slightly and the amount of body movement you put into it. Guard against stiffening yourself up; relax and hit right down and through the ball with a firm hand action and keep the clubface square at impact.

There is a widespread tendency to under-club on mid-iron approach shots, either because players have a false impression of their ability, or because they don't really appreciate how far they hit the ball with each particular club. It is well worth spending a little time on the practice ground hitting shots with these clubs and measuring how far you hit them. This will give you a much clearer idea of your capabilities on the course.

Play the mid-irons from the centre of the feet and make sure that the hands continue down and through the ball towards the target.

The 5 and 6 irons are also often used for getting out of rough which is not too thick. The principles are exactly the same as for any other shot, but remember that the longer grass tends to wrap itself round the clubhead and close the face at impact. It is a good idea to aim a little right of the target on these shots.

THE SHORT IRONS

No matter how good a golfer may be, there are bound to be many occasions when he will miss the green with his second shot but, if he really is a first-class player, this need not affect his score very much. The good player will be able to produce short approach or recovery shots that will give him every chance of making a single putt and saving his par figures.

The short irons – the 7, 8, 9 and wedge – are used from approximately a hundred and twenty yards in from the flag and can be made to execute a tremendously varied range of shots. Perhaps the most dramatic of these shots is the high-flying pitch, where the object is to land the ball on the green near the flag and stop it as quickly as possible by imparting backspin on the ball. But the pitch is not always the most successful stroke. If the ground is fairly dry and you are only a few yards off the green with no obstacles to negotiate, it is usually more accurate to play a pitch and run shot, where the ball is simply plopped on to the edge of the green and allowed to run up to the flag. This, of course, is a much lower-flighted type of golf shot.

On a full pitch shot from, say, 120 yards, most average golfers would use a 7 iron, an 8 iron from 110 yards, a 9 iron from approximately ninety yards, and a wedge from eighty yards. Of course, this again varies from person to person. Some people have the ability to hit a 9 iron 120 or 130 yards. It is just one of those things that you have to discover for yourself.

The pitch is basically a hand and arm shot with practically no hip pivot and little footwork – just a little 'give' in the knees is quite sufficient. The ball should be played from the centre of

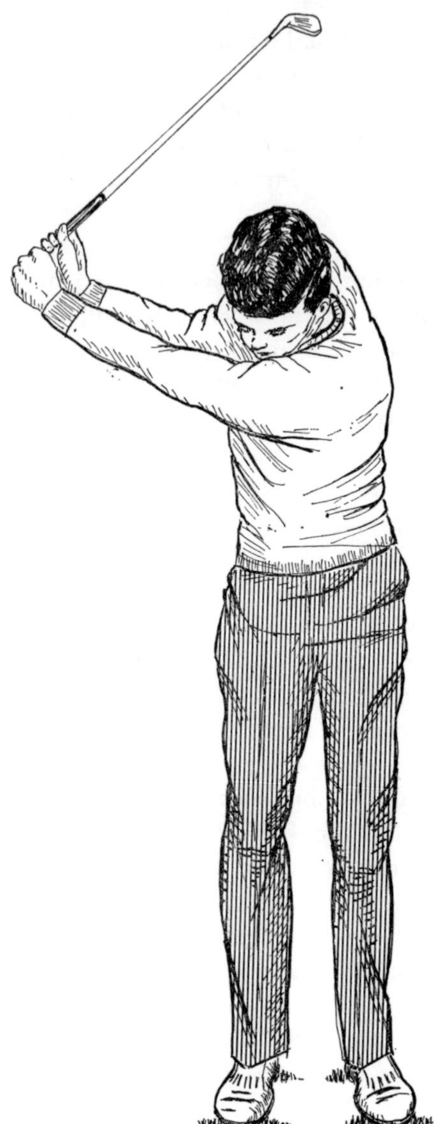

FIG. 11

A. Plenty of wrist action and good length of swing with lofted pitch shot.

B. Chip, or pitch and run, shot more 'punchy'; backswing shorter with less wrist action.

the feet which are only a few inches apart – generally speaking, the shorter the shot, the closer together the feet should be. This cuts out any unnecessary body action from the swing.

As with every other golf shot, the hands must play their important part and hit down and through the ball to produce the ball/turf sequence but, with the pitch shot, the hand action is slightly different. With all the other clubs we have concentrated on taking the club back in a one-piece action – clubhead, hands, arms and shoulders all moving as one unit. With the pitch shot there should be a much earlier cocking of the wrists – almost as soon as the club is started on the backswing, in fact. This produces a much steeper swing, both up and down, which gives the shot greater height and helps to impart the tremendous backspin required to stop the ball almost dead in its tracks when it pitches.

Taking the club back so that the hands are at shoulder-height is quite sufficient backswing for a full pitch shot. The important thing to remember on the way down is that the later the wrists unleash into the ball the better and the more backspin will be created.

Short pitches can be quite delicate, but that doesn't mean that you can ever afford to play them sloppily. They must be crisply executed with the hands firmly in control of the clubface all the time. If you try to play these shots out with the necessary firmness, you run the risk of fluffing behind the ball.

The wedge is unlike any other club in the bag. It has the greatest loft on the face and also a wide 'skid' sole which will force its way through long grass or bounce through bunker sand. It is the club most used by professionals for those wonderful little pitch shots to the flag that they play so expertly when they have to pop the ball over a bunker or a mound.

The right hand should be placed well over the shaft for this type of shot so that the clubface is held open at impact. Using a narrow stance, position the ball just inside the left heel and try to take the club back slightly on the outside groove so that you are swinging slightly across the ball. This imparts backspin which stops the shot quickly on pitching, as does the early cocking of the wrists. You can afford to use quite a bit of wrist flick in the impact area as this helps to get the ball up quickly.

These wedge pitches can be wonderful stroke savers around the greenif they are properly executed, but the only way that players like Arnold Palmer and Jack Nicklaus are able to put them so close to the hole so often is by constant practice. It is a shot which requires good judgement, delicacy and a tremendous amount of hard work.

Where there is no obstacle between you and the flag, and there is not too much ground to cover before reaching the putting surface, the pitch and run shot can be used to great effect. Depending on the conditions, you could use any club from a 3 iron to a 9 iron for these little shots, but a 7 iron is an excellent club for the purpose, and that is the one I would recommend beginners to use.

The object of the shot is to pop the ball just on the putting surface and then let it run on to the flag. Only practice and your judgment will tell you how hard to hit the ball to reach any given target, but this soon comes with a little experience.

The technique for the pitch and run is quite simple, yet it is all too easy to fluff the shot if you don't play it firmly. The feet should be only a few inches apart, with the ball in the centre. Hold the club halfway down the grip with the hands slightly ahead of the ball. Now slowly and smoothly take the club back from the ball with no body movement and very little wrist action. On the downswing, the hands and arms push through the ball towards the hole without any attempt at flicking the ball into the air. The loft on the club will take care of that. It is absolutely vital on these delicate little shots that the head must remain perfectly still, and that you watch the ball like a hawk. If you take your eye off it for a moment, the odds are that you will mishit the shot.

BUNKER SHOTS

Bunkers are no longer the dreaded hazards that they used to be. The invention of the sand wedge during the 1930s has helped everybody to become bunker 'experts' – as long as they have been prepared to practise the technique. The sand wedge is similar to the pitching wedge (indeed, many clubs do double duty) but it generally has slightly more loft and an even broader sole which is designed to 'splash' through the top surface of sand without becoming embedded in it.

The first thing you must remember when you step into a sand trap is that you are not permitted by the rules of golf to ground the club – even when you are addressing the ball, you must hold the sole of the club clear of the sand.

Your object is to take sand and ball together, which means that the club must start splashing through the sand *behind* the ball. You play this shot in much the same way as you would a normal wedge pitch – open stance, quick wrist cock, take the club back on the outside, make sure that the face is open on the downswing, follow through. But this is the one and only shot in golf where you do not watch the ball at all. Because you want the club to enter the sand two inches behind the ball, that is the point you must watch.

This 'splash' shot, as it is called, is ideal for green-side bunkers, and with a little practice it is possible to become extremely accurate. The top tournament professionals have no fear at all of bunkers round a green because they are sufficiently confident that they can get down in two strokes from sand nearly every time. When you watch a good bunker player, notice the speed at which he swings the club. It is very slow and unhurried – almost in slow motion – with no apparent attempt at hitting the ball hard. There is absolutely no suggestion that he is trying to scoop the ball out of the bunker; if he did that, he would be playing his next stroke from the same spot.

Fairway bunkers need not necessarily mean a completely wasted shot. Obviously the sensible thing is to make sure first of all that you can get out but, if you decide that you can get out of trouble and hit a long shot at the same time, don't feel afraid to try it. Select a club that will get the ball clear of the bunker face and take up your address position so that the ball is slightly back of centre. This will ensure that you hit the ball before the sand which is absolutely imperative if you are going to hit the shot successfully. Get a firm footing in the sand, because with your full swing it is very easy to slip and lose balance. Then simply concentrate on swinging away smoothly and hitting down on the ball before the sand. Properly hit, this shot will travel just as far as the same iron played from the fairway.

PUTTING

Putting is the most personal part of the game and I leave it to you to select a putter that you like the feel of, and to develop a style that is both comfortable and efficient.

However, there are one or two factors that are common to nearly all good putters and I mention them for your guidance. Most consistent holers-out have their feet quite close together, with the knees bent and relaxed, arms and elbows fairly close in to the body. Generally, they position the ball near the left toe, but invariably they keep their shoulders still during the stroke, and their eyes are directly over the ball.

There are a variety of grips used in putting, but one of the most popular is the reverse overlap, where the index finger of the left hand overlaps the little finger of the right. This means that all the fingers of the right hand are on the putter grip, and the right hand is completely in control of the stroke.

The object of the putting swing is to take the club squarely away from the ball on the backswing and squarely into and through the ball on the downswing. On such a short movement this sounds a relatively simple operation, but it has driven many great players almost to the brink of despair. Like everything else in golf, putting requires practice and more practice.

I don't intend to say any more about putting because everybody must evolve a method for themselves; the important thing is that it must be comfortable and relaxed. There hasn't been

FIG. 12 A and B

Although putting is a very personal matter, good putters follow certain principles: position

a man yet who could hole putts while he felt stiff or tensed up. You will discover that putting is one per cent method and ninety-nine per cent psychological. The putter is the club you

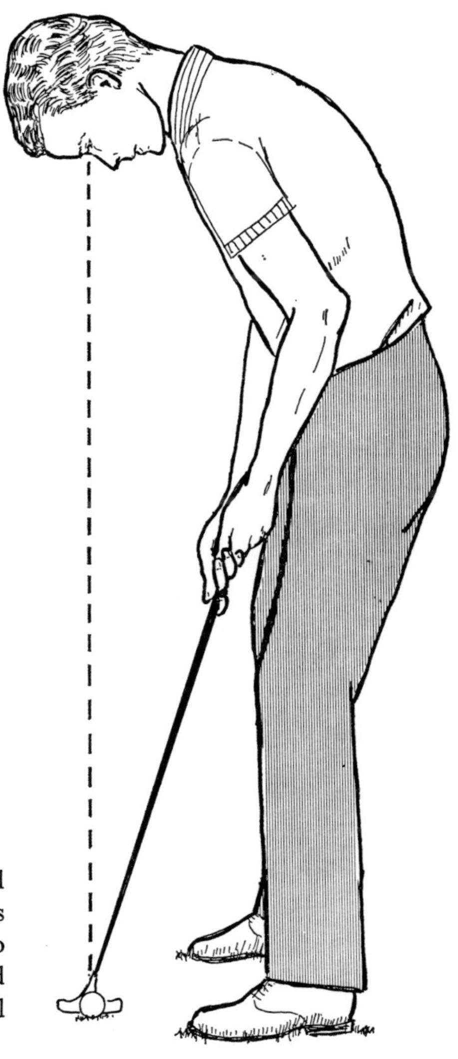

should be relaxed and comfortable, with knees flexed and arms close to body and with head immediately over ball *always*.

use most often in a round of golf, so it is well worth your while making friends with it on the practice green. Golf doesn't finish once you've got the ball on to the putting surface; it finishes when the ball is safely in the hole.

HOW SHOULD MY SWING DEVELOP?

The golf swing is rather like a finger-print. It is a personal thing, and no matter where you go or how many golfers you watch, you will never see anybody else using a swing that is identical in every respect with yours. There may be similarities, but never a carbon copy.

If I were to take twenty young men of average proportions and teach every one of them exactly the same things and complete orthodoxy, I could guarantee that by the time I had finished I might have twenty fairly accomplished golfers, but I would certainly have twenty different golf swings.

The reason is that everybody is built slightly differently. One man might have strong hands, another weak. One might have powerful legs, another not so powerful, and so on. Then there is the difference in interpretation. What I tell one pupil might mean something entirely different to another.

Everybody who has had a chance of watching them would agree that Arnold Palmer, Jack Nicklaus and Gary Player are all great champions of the game, giants of the modern era of golfers. Yet do they swing alike? Not in the least. The only thing they have in common is the ability to bring the clubhead square and amazingly fast into the back of the ball.

Naturally, the thing that mostly determines the way you will swing a golf club is your physique and physical potentialities, but also one's temperament has a lot to do with it.

For more than thirty years Dai Rees has been a credit to the British professional golfers, both as a man and as a player. Dai is only a small chap and, being a voluble Welshman, he walks and talks quickly; in fact, he does practically everything quickly. It would be quite out of character for Dai to have a slow, smooth golf swing. The swing he has is much more characteristic – fairly quick, with a short, compact backswing. Dai tries to make up for his lack of inches by punching the ball as hard as he can.

Big strong people usually lead life at a slower rate altogether. They walk and talk more slowly, are less excitable and are generally pretty placid sort of folk. This really decides what sort of golf swing they will develop. Generally, it is a longer, slower, rhythmical action. Sam Snead, who stands six feet two, is a perfect example of this category. He probably possesses the most perfect golf swing in the business, poetry in motion, which is slow and rhythmic from start to finish.

How long should your backswing be? This depends on several things, of course – how supple you are, how tall you are, etc. – but the backswing should be no longer than you can control, and no longer than it needs to be to create maximum clubhead speed at impact.

Jimmy Adams, a top-class player of my era, was able to pivot very easily, even though he didn't raise his heel from the ground at all. He had a tremendously long swing, with the shaft going way beyond the horizontal at the top, yet he was able to keep his hands completely in control of the club all the time.

Doug Sanders, on the other hand, has decided that he can gain maximum power from very little pivot and with the clubhead getting only slightly higher than his shoulders at the top. Certainly, Doug manages to hit the ball very straight with this short sharp swing which has earned him thousands of dollars on the American circuit.

Whether ultimately you develop a full swing, the beginner should concentrate during his first year or so on mastering the three-quarter swing, where the hands are taken back to about shoulder height. He will find this swing easy to control and there is less room for anything to go wrong. Once you can hit the ball consistently with this action you can try lengthening it a bit at a time so that you are building up your control all the while. The thing to remember on the full backswing is that the left hand must never be allowed to open so that the club is moving about in the hands. If this starts to happen all control is lost and there is no hope of bringing the clubface into the ball squarely. The only solution is either to shorten the swing or build up the strength of the last three fingers of the left hand so that they won't open at the critical moment.

As I've already explained, the tempo of the swing depends largely on the player's physique and temperament, but it's absolutely wrong to swing the club back fast; I would much rather see a person swing the club back smoothly with a one-piece action and then accelerate into the ball on the downswing.

On the other hand, the backswing shouldn't be too slow because the change in tempo is so great between the backswing and the downswing that there is almost bound to be a snatch at the top.

One position where the top golfers vary is at the top of the swing. Some have the left wrist slightly cupped, while others even have the wrist slightly convex at the top of the swing. This last example is used by only one or two professionals who have tremendously strong hands, and who are able to practise a great deal, and it is not recommended for the beginner.

I don't believe in over-complicating the golf swing. While the position of the left wrist makes interesting comparisons between the top players, I advise my pupils that if they stick to the orthodox two or two-and-a-half knuckle grip, they will be in the right position at the top of the swing – either with the left wrist straight or slightly cupped, depending on the strength of a player's hands. The most important thing is that it should feel comfortable and that the golfer feels he can bring the clubface square into the back of the ball. You can always check whether you are in a good position by swinging the club back to the top and then checking that the shaft is pointing straight at the target and not to the right or to the left.

There have been good players who have confounded this rule. Bobby Locke was a wonderful example because, at the top of his swing, the club shaft always pointed way over to the rough on the right. Lloyd Mangrum, a fine American player of a year or two ago, was the complete opposite: his shaft pointed well to the left of the target. But then Locke was a tremendous hooker of the ball and Mangrum hit every shot with fade. For ordinary mortals the position in between these two is the safest bet.

Pupils often ask whether they should try to swing the club flat or upright. I don't think it is possible to have an upright backswing; the difference is merely that some swings are flatter than others. The longer the club you use, the flatter your swing is bound to be. If, for instance, you stood half a mile away ırom the ball, then your swing would be very flat indeed and if you stood forty-four inches away from it, it would also be flat, but if you were to address the ball only an inch or so away from your toes, then the swing would have to be upright. Of course, it isn't possible to play from any of these positions, and the ball is usually eighteen or twenty inches away from the feet. Thus, with a short club, the swing is slightly more upright than it would be with a driver.

For the more powerful shots the flatter swing is best because if you try to lift the club up into a more upright position, there is a real danger of putting the clubhead on the outside groove. If you take the club back with the arms and shoulders working together, it will naturally go back on a slightly inside plane, which will mean that you are in a position to hit the ball with an inside-to-out action which helps to produce a slight draw on the ball, which is struck with right to left spin.

A lot of people are afraid to turn their shoulders because they think it will cause a flat swing: not at all; it will simply create an 'inside swing' and this is the sort of action that suits most golfers. Don't be afraid of turning your shoulders on the backswing and taking the club back on the inside; this is ideal.

The longer the club the flatter the swing will be. It will be flattest with a driver and most upright with a wedge. This is what helps to keep the ball down low on your tee shots, but flight it high quickly on pitch shots.

The modern technique is to hit all your power shots low and with that touch of draw that helps them to roll another twenty yards. The Irish professional Harry Bradshaw used to swing the club back right round his body into a very flat position when he hit the ball off the tee. He was so confident with this method that the ball used to fly smack down the middle every time with just a little draw at the end to give him those extra yards.

FIG. 13

Length of club dictates plane of swing: full swing with driver must be on flatter plane than with wedge or short lofted iron.

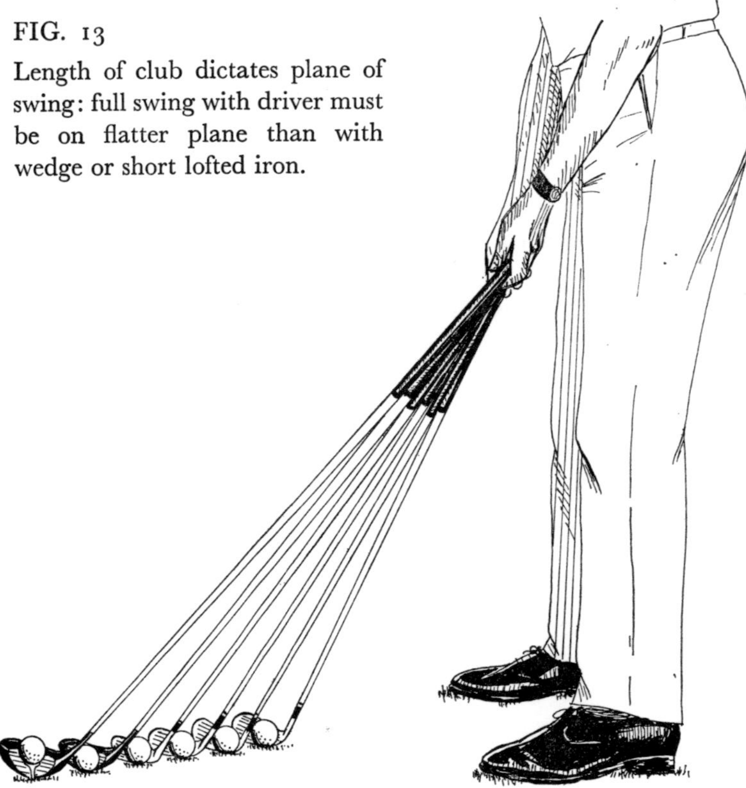

No golfer can swing exactly the same with every club in the bag. One talks glibly about the groove of the swing, but in fact there is a different groove for every club. It's mechanically impossible for the groove of the driver to be exactly the same as for the wedge. Apart from the difference in the lengths of the shaft, the ball is positioned differently to start with. But let me make this perfectly clear: you should not *feel* that you are swinging the club any differently. Don't be confused into thinking that because the grooves are different for each club you have to alter your action. The swing will slip into the different grooves quite naturally.

I don't like to see anyone trying to make his swing upright because nearly always this puts the club on the outside. The swing on the long shots should be slightly flat and on the inside.

As the years go by and your golfing experience becomes wider, you will make slight alterations to your swing, changes that help you to hit the ball better. You may tend towards a slightly shut stance, you may find that you hit the ball straighter by slightly altering the position of your hands on the grip. There are all manner of little idiosyncrasies you may develop, but for the time being, I suggest that you follow orthodox teaching and develop a sound knowledge of the golf swing. I'm sure you won't go far wrong.

SOME FALLACIES

Over the years golf teaching has gathered round it so much dogma and so many catch-phrases that are not only confusing to the beginner, but sometimes downright incorrect! I have already tried to explain that it is practically impossible to 'keep the head still' during the golf swing, and what the people who so glibly give this advice should really say is 'watch the ball'.

Another favourite piece of advice between club golfers is 'stop swaying'. I have tried to impress on you that, to get maximum power into the shot, there must be a full transference of weight from the left foot to the right on the backswing, and from the right foot to the left during the downswing. Just try doing that without swaying! It isn't possible.

Unfortunately, this catch-phrase is so widely accepted among golfers that many of them throw their swings completely out of gear in an effort *not* to sway. Often I see people who are so afraid of swaying to the right on the backswing that they tilt their weight *completely* on the left foot so that when they start coming down, these golfers are unable to shift any more weight to the left and, as they can't move forward, they have to throw their weight on to the right foot. In fact, they are swaying forward on the backswing and backward on the downswing. Christy O'Connor, the top Irish professional and one of the best players in these islands for many a year, moves his weight beautifully and has a *very* noticeable sway. His action is smooth, powerful and well balanced, and his sway does not prevent him from taking the club right through into a fine finishing position. His sway is perfectly under control and he hits every shot with the correct ball/turf sequence.

Christy told me many years ago that he learned to play iron shots off the sand of Galway Bay. If you try it, you will soon discover that you have to hit the ball before the sand every time. If you hit the sand first, you lose power and fluff the shot completely.

As far as I'm concerned, swaying into the ball is not a fault at all – it's a very necessary part of the swing.

Another catch-phrase that is often used is 'keep your head behind the ball'. Nonsense! If you are transferring your weight properly, your whole body must move into the shot, including your head.

Try throwing a ball, keeping your weight absolutely still. You will find that you can only throw it about fifteen yards because you've only got the power of your arm behind it. But if you put your weight on the right foot and, as you throw the ball, move that weight through at the same time, you will throw it very much farther. Now see if you can do that without moving your head forward at the same time.

If you want to get real power into a golf shot, you've got to move about. If it were essential that you shouldn't sway during a golf stroke, all you would have to do is put your feet close together. It would stop you swaying all right but it would also cut most of the power out of your shot straight away. It would prevent you from getting that mass movement into the shot that creates velocity.

If your feet are correctly placed and doing their job properly, swaying into the ball won't make you lose your balance. Some years ago I gave Douglas Bader a lesson; he, as you know, lost both his legs in a flying accident just before the war. I watched him hit one or two shots and decided that he was standing much too close to the ball. I told him to get farther away from it so that he had plenty of room to attack the back of the ball. 'I can't do that,' he said, 'I shall fall over'. A little nervous at first, he gave it a try, and hit some of the best golf shots of his life! By giving himself a little more room, he was able to bring his whole body weight into the shot – and he didn't fall over, so why should you?

There is a lot of talk nowadays about the 'long right arm'. This means that the right arm is perfectly straight just after impact and remains straight for as long as possible through the ball. Once again, this is absolute rubbish! There are many more important things to think about than keeping your right arm straight, and the effort of trying to hit the ball with a straight right arm causes one to hit too early. When you are at the top of the backswing, the right arm is bent. In order to get it straight at or just after impact, you are almost forced to throw the elbow into the shot. In throwing the elbow you almost invariably throw the clubhead.

My old friend Max Faulkner, who won the Open Championship in 1951, was once asked to pose for some photographs. Eventually, the photographer got what he wanted, a picture of Max with his right arm straight somewhere beyond impact. But it had taken Maxie about thirty strokes before he managed to get into that position, and he had hit some terrible shots while trying to do it!

I do not believe that you can possibly have good delayed wrist action if you are trying to achieve the so-called 'long right arm'. In forty years of playing, teaching and watching the game, I am convinced that delayed wrist action, or late hitting, is an absolute 'must' if you want to be a really good player. Every golfer should aim at trying to hit the ball and then the turf with every club in the bag – even the driver.

David Thomas, probably the longest hitter of a golf ball in the world today, has always impressed me with his ability to hit the ball very late. I remember watching him hit a drive with a very deep-faced club and the ball perched on a high tee. He hit the ball down and through with his driver, although, of course, he didn't actually take a divot. The ball started very low and travelled for about two hundred and fifty yards before it started to climb – and then it went on for another 100 yards!

He had hit this shot with very late wrist action and the result was tremendous to watch.

Make no mistake: anyone who says that delayed wrist action is only for the good player is talking a lot of rubbish. I believe that late hitting should be taught from the very first lesson.

There are still many people who seem to think, that because you're hitting late, you must be hitting the ball with the face open. This, again, is nonsense. What is to stop you closing the clubface slightly at impact and still hitting late?

If you watch Arnold Palmer hitting those 1 irons of his, you will notice that he takes the divot long after he has hit the ball. This means that he hit the shot with a descending blow and with the hands ahead of the clubhead at impact. Do these shots slice out to the right because his face was open? Not a bit of it. They fly like bullets straight at the target – simply because he has kept the clubface square. At any major tournament you will notice two things: the best players hit the ball late, and they hit it with a hooded clubface which produces a slight draw. Neil Coles is a wonderful example of this method of striking.

You've got to bring your hands down fast from the top of the swing while leaving the clubhead behind. Transferring the weight to the left foot and moving your body into the ball helps a lot. You want to get the feeling that you're almost hitting the ball straight down into the ground, and you can afford to do this very much more than you think. You will know when you've achieved the proper late hit, for the ball will come off the clubface with a sharp crack and you will have the sensation that the ball has almost been squeezed into the ground by the clubface. There's no better feeling in golf, but I'm afraid it's the sort of feeling that so many players never know.

Another very damaging catch-phrase is 'let the club do the work'. This piece of advice is freely given to all golfers by their brethren and, while it may be given in all good faith, it is just another example of how little the average golfer understands the golf game. If you're going to 'let the club do the work' then what are *you* doing there? Of course the club won't do the work for you; it is up to you to make the hands do the work and to make the hands control the clubface all the time. If you 'let the club do the work' your swing will become sloppy and without control.

A favourite catch-phrase with all golfers is 'take the club back slowly'. What they really mean is 'take the club back smoothly'. If your backswing is very slow, you feel that you have to snatch at the top to get any power into the stroke. You have not built any rhythm into your swing. It is much better if you determine to swing the club back smoothly and at a more natural tempo, and then really let fly on the downswing.

All too often I hear one golfer saying to another: 'Keep your left arm stiff.' Of course, they don't really mean that, because stiffness in any part of the body is a shocking fault. With a stiff left arm you will only be able to push at the ball without getting any real power or zip into the shot. Try to keep the left arm straight, but never, never allow it to become stiff.

When a golfer hooks the ball badly, you can often hear him muttering to himself: 'I must have used too much right hand.' This is one of those pieces of nonsense that have been handed down through the years and have become generally accepted. It just isn't possible to use too much right hand, and one famous professional was once quoted as saying: 'I wish I had three right hands. I'd use all of them as hard as I could.'

You can easily prove to yourself the importance of the right hand by taking a few golf balls on to the practice ground and hitting some with the left hand only and the rest with the right hand. You will find that you have much greater power and precision. It's the same in tennis. You can hit a forehand much more powerfully than a backhand.

These are just a few of the dangerous catch-phrases that have become ingrained in golf teaching. There are plenty more, of course, but these are some of the worst examples that you can hear any weekend at any golf club. Read over them again and determine that you will not take any notice of people who offer you these little titbits of advice. It will give you a much clearer mind on the course and help you to swing the club much more freely into the back of the ball.

BALANCE AND RHYTHM

If you follow closely the principles I have tried to lay down in this book, you will find that your own natural rhythm soon develops in the swing. People are often accused of swinging the club too fast, but speed is not a fault; the real fault is jerkiness in the swing, and it is very easy to develop a jerk or a snatch at the top by swinging back too *slowly*. When you watch most of the world's top professionals on television, you will notice that they make no attempt to swing the club slowly, but they are producing a smooth flowing action in one complete unit. It is not a series of actions welded together, but one complete *form*.

I am very fond of seeing a good-looking style as long as it is allied to a good strong hand action. The sweetest swing in the world is no use at all unless it is controlled by a strong pair of hands that can guide the clubface squarely into the ball. I like to see the classic follow-through position from my pupils – fingers firm on the club, hands high, belt-buckle facing the hole, weight on the left foot and the right side just gently balanced on the tip of the right toe. This suggests that the player has used his hands and feet properly and has kept himself balanced throughout the swing.

With professionals, it's slightly different. They usually have one swing when they are posing for the camera, the 'gallery' swing, and another, the tournament swing, when they are in the thick of the battle playing for money. The finish to the tournament swing is shorter and tighter, and the pros are hanging on to the shot like grim death. They can't afford to hit any shot slackly. While they may lose balance a little once the ball is on its way, you can be sure that they were perfectly balanced at the moment of impact.

The professional and the experienced player knows how to use his feet and legs properly in order to keep his balance, but this is something that the raw beginner has to learn over a period. Using a long club on a driving range can be dangerous unless you concentrate hard on all you have learned and try to hit the ball smoothly with the hands. Too many driving range customers seem to think that they've got to hit the cover off the ball with a driver. They most probably have the ball too far away from them and are setting themselves up to it badly. They might not have their feet the right width apart and they might either be reaching for the ball or have it too close to them. If you take a violent slash at it under these conditions, you are bound to lose balance. It also takes quite a bit of time before one is able to judge accurately how near or how far one should stand from the ball and how wide apart the feet should be.

I try to instil rhythm and balance into a pupil's swing when he comes to me for that crucial first lesson. By giving him a shortish club and asking him to simply swing it back and forth, back and forth in a continuous movement, slowly building up the basic footwork and weight transference, he very soon starts to feel the rhythm of the swing and how he should feel balanced. The feet are the key to balance because they control the knee action and the knee action controls the hip action. Soon it becomes quite natural because in the first instance the pupil has not tried to cope with bad footwork or over-reaching for the ball.

As the strength in the hands develops, the swing becomes that little bit faster, and the pupil starts to hit the ball a little farther. However, no new golfer should start trying to hit the ball very far for at least the first year. Until he has a sound grasp of the principles of the game, he should not try to knock the cover off the ball, as he will only succeed in slashing at it, losing his rhythm and balance. If the beginner simply concentrates on developing good footwork and hand action, he will soon get the feel of the swing and, as his power increases, so the force of his swing can increase.

One of the worst things that can upset a player's balance is the insistence these days that the arc of the swing should be made as wide as possible. My opinion is that if you transfer your weight normally and keep the left arm straight, there is no need to try and make the arc any wider. You certainly don't want to start pushing the clubhead out just to increase your arc by six inches. This is bound to give you a stiff movement on the backswing and if there is stiffness in the swing, there can never be a smooth rhythm and good balance. It can cause other problems too. If you watch a player trying to stretch his arms back as far as they will go, more often than not the head will dip down. He is in that awful position of having the head too low at the top of the backswing and must pull his head up and out of the way as he hits the ball and this can lead to all manner of trouble. A person can move the head slightly from side to side, but it must *never* move up or down. I am not a believer in trying to develop a very wide arc. The best swing is the orthodox one that feels most comfortable to you. Only then will you have good rhythm and balance.

THINK BEFORE YOU PLAY

They say that golf is ten per cent physical and ninety per cent mental and there is probably a good deal of truth in that. Given a person of normal physical qualifications who is prepared to do a little hard work, in time I could make him into a pretty good swinger of the club. If he was then prepared to practise a good deal, he could develop into a good *striker* of the ball, but unless he had the right approach and mental attitude to golf, he could never become the complete golfer and a good competitor.

Only the trials and tribulations of playing golf under all kinds of conditions will properly attune you to the game mentally. It will teach you calmness in a crisis, strength of character, determination, resilience, and how to get on with other people. Golf teaches you more about yourself than any other sport, and it can either bring out the best or the worst in people. There isn't a professional in the world who can teach you how to cope with yourself mentally – even though a good professional combines his actual teaching of technique with a little psychology.

I can only advise you that you will never play well if you can't control your temper – and sometimes golf can be the most frustrating of games – nor will you play your best until you develop that competitive urge to win.

Where I can help you a little is by explaining how you should approach each individual shot and what you ought to be thinking about just before and during your stroke.

So many golf shots are badly hit because the player hasn't stopped for a moment to give the circumstances due consideration. Instead, he has just walked up to the ball and hit it 'somewhere towards the green'. Often his mind is elsewhere or he's wondering what the people in front are doing so long on the green. This time could more usefully be spent in preparing himself to play the shot on hand.

If you have an important shot to play, the best thing to concentrate on is watching the ball closely all the time. Convince yourself that if you watch it like a hawk it really does bring about greater co-ordination between hand and eye and helps you to hit the shot in the centre of the clubface more consistently.

Perhaps you have weighed up the shot carefully and can see that you only have a very narrow target to aim at. Under these circumstances, far too many golfers become rigid and stiff in the legs. They are afraid to use their feet because they think that if they let the left heel come off the ground, they will sway badly and knock the ball off line. On the contrary, if you are stiff in the legs, you are far more likely to drop that ball into a green-side bunker than if you simply relax and let the feet and legs do their job properly. The more freely you swing the club through to the hole, the straighter your flight is likely to be, so don't let a tight shot make you tighten your swing.

A great many players do not think enough about how they are gripping the club when they step up to the shot. You should check that your grip is sound every time you take a club out of the bag. It's so easy to slip into bad habits without noticing. Perhaps the left hand has crept too far under the shaft or the right hand is too much on top. Make sure that the Vs are always towards a point between your chin and right shoulder, and no matter how tense the situation may be, be careful not to grip the club too tightly – firmly, yes, but don't squeeze the life out of it. This will only produce tension in your wrists and forearms.

If you grip the club correctly every time, you will halve your number of bad shots.

Try to get a mental picture of your hands whipping into the

ball. This will help you to keep the clubface under control all the time and make sure that you connect with the centre of the clubface. Many club golfers just swing the clubface at the ball and hope that the two will meet in the right spot. More often than not, they won't – unless *you* make sure that they do.

Should you play the shots quietly and safely, or should you always try to play an attacking shot? To my mind an attacking shot is always the safest. It can be very dangerous to play with a 'spared' swing because the hand action tends to become a little sloppy and you will often either pull the ball to the left or push it out to the right of the target. Even the best players don't like these 'soft' shots, although the top professionals are quite capable of playing them. The average weekend player is much better off playing a firm 6 iron, say, than trying to 'baby' a 5. It will give him so much more authority in his swing and in the hand action.

You never hit shots on the course quite as well as you hit them on the practice ground because there is always the bunker on the left, those irritating people in front, and 'this is where I hit a bad one yesterday'. There is always a little more apprehension of hitting a bad shot. Try to remove these thoughts from your mind by thinking simply: 'I'm going to swing the club well and watch the ball. I'm going to attack it with the centre of the clubface.' Invariably, you play a much better stroke than if you let your fears intrude in your mind.

Club golfers never plan their rounds properly. They could learn a thing or two from watching Jack Nicklaus play a practice round before the start of the tournament. Jack measures distances at every hole from various prominent landmarks, and then decides which way to play each hole. He might put the tee shot down the right-hand side at one hole, because it leaves him with the easiest approach shot to the green, and then he might play well over to the left at the next.

You may not have the ability of a Jack Nicklaus, but it is important to plan the way you play every hole with regard to your individual capabilities. You must first decide what you can do with your power and your particular flight on the ball. Then you must have confidence in your ability to perform the task you have set yourself.

When you are studying an approach shot, don't just think to yourself: 'I can hit it on to the green from here.' Have a good look at the green again and take note of where the flag is placed. It may be close to a bunker on the right, so the sensible thing to do would be play for the middle of the green to the left of the hole – while you may not be so close to the stick, at least you are giving yourself a putting chance rather than having to play your next out of sand.

The flag may be right at the back of the green, so if you judge that you need a 5 iron to put you in the centre of the putting surface, you might well need a 4 iron to get up to the flag in this particular position. On the other hand, it might be at the front, in which case you will need a 6 iron. Judging approach shots carefully can make a tremendous difference to your scores, and give you plenty of chances at holeable putts.

The American professionals are the greatest pressure putters in the world. Most of them play the stroke with a short sharp attacking rap, and it is not very often that you see an American leave the ball short of the hole – they give it a chance of going in every time they step on to the putting green. I believe, as a general rule, in attack on every shot on the golf course, not least on the putting green, but there may be times when this is not the wisest move. If, for instance, the hole has been cut into a sharp slope, and there is a danger of the ball running away and leaving you a difficult second putt, then the sensible thing to do, obviously, is to lag the first putt up safely to the hole so that you have only a tap-in for your second.

While we are talking about putting, remember this: when the pressure's on and you've got a difficult putt to make, your head tends to swing like a metronome. Without becoming rigid, try to keep the head still throughout the stroke and focus your complete attention on the ball.

The longer you play this great game of golf, the more you will appreciate how important the mental side of golf is to the player. You are for ever assailed by different stresses and strains but in time your experience will help you to overcome them. You will not only become a much better player when this happens; it will also help you to develop into a better person with a clearer insight into yourself.

GOLF FOR THE NOT-SO-YOUNG

With the pressures of modern life and the demands on so many people's time, many golfers are not in a position to settle back and relax until they are over forty years of age. For the majority of these people, golf can never be the game that it is to the youngster. Older folk will not have the suppleness or the strength to get maximum power into the shot, and it is doubtful that they will have the mustard-keenness to improve. Even so, this category of player can be taught to play quite a proficient game that will still give him many hours of happiness on the golf course.

The swing principles are exactly the same as for anyone else. You do not need the strength of a Samson to play golf my way, nor do you need the flexibility of a spring. Nevertheless, middle-aged golfers have particular problems of their own, and as it is now forty years since I came into the game, I feel well qualified to help them.

The thing about almost all middle-aged golfers who are just coming into the game is that they tend to be very stiff in the legs and have hands unprepared for the task of swinging a golf club.

Time and again, I have watched such people swinging, and on the backswing the right leg is rammed back stiffly, and on the downswing the left leg is pushed straight and stiff. When I tell them that they must bend the knees and relax the legs properly, everything relaxes to the point of limpness, even their grip on the club. What the not-so-young golfer has to try to achieve is an aggressive hand action and a relaxed leg action.

These golfers also tend to have stiff wrists, and they must practise swinging the club in order to get more flexibility into the wrist action. They are often a little afraid of letting fly with their hands and, instead, try to guide the ball down the fairway. They are nervous of whipping the clubhead into the back of the ball as they come into the shot.

To get over these problems, my advice is to squeeze the grip of the club quite firmly in the fingers while retaining as much wrist action as possible through the ball. Get the legs really relaxed so that at the top of the backswing the right knee is slightly bent – not pushed back stiff and locked there. If you do lock the right leg there's a danger of freezing the right side completely, and then the only way you can get the club down to the ball is by rolling the right shoulder on the downswing. Of course, this is a dreadful fault and can cause either badly pulled or badly sliced shots.

If you feel that your legs are too stiff, I suggest that you try swinging without a ball, keeping the knees well bent. Just swing the club back and forth in one continuous movement, as you did in that first lesson. This is the best way I know of making any golfer relax completely.

Beware of relaxing your grip on the club, whatever the length of shot you are going to play. Try to get the hands coming through the impact zone fast by using plenty of wrist action.

As I say, many golfers, and this doesn't only apply to the middle-aged, are so afraid of knocking the ball off line that they simply wave or push the club at the ball with no speed through the shot. The way these folk play, they couldn't crack an egg, let alone hit the ball past the 200-yard marker. It's no good fitting maximum control to minimum power. What you've got to do is develop maximum power and then learn to control it.

This was brought home to me when I was at a women's golf tournament quite recently. The girls from the Continent obviously derived great pleasure from being able to hit the ball a long way and, because they had such power at their command, they were not in the least concerned when they knocked the odd shot off line. They knew they had the strength of hand action to get the ball out of any trouble. On the other hand, the British women in this tournament were very short in comparison. One told me: 'I may not be long, but I'm very, very straight.' She thought it was quite clever to be able to hit the ball straight. It isn't at all – golf shots need to be long *and* straight.

The middle-aged golfer may never hit the ball as far as Jack Nicklaus – or even Catherine Lacoste – but he must develop his hand action to the full and hit it as far as his capabilities will allow. Certainly, hitting the ball a good distance makes the game a lot more fun.

Most middle-aged golfers don't use their feet enough. Don't be flat-footed; let your feet work – it will help to keep those legs from getting stiff. Make sure that the left heel lifts an inch or two on the backswing, and then swing right through on to the left foot. It all helps to increase clubhead speed.

Many golfers who are in the not-so-young category are still using clubs that might have suited them twenty years ago. The shafts are probably a little too stiff, and if you've had the clubs for any period of time, it's almost certain that the grips are slippery. Golf clubs are pretty advanced weapons these days, and you must treat them as friends. They have been designed to help you, not to hinder. Many club golfers are using clubs that are too stiff in the shaft and too heavy in the head.

For the over fifties I think it is a very good idea to give the A shaft a try. This is a bit whippier than the regular shaft and gives you an extra little bit of zing as you come into the ball. It may well be that you could now use a slightly thicker grip because the fingers have lost some of their old flexibility – and make sure that the grips are always tacky; it makes them so much easier to hold, whether you have great strength in your fingers or not.

One of the great consolations of golf is that it is a game you don't have to stop playing at thirty. It can give you endless pleasure well into old age. The middle-aged men and women are the pillars of the golf club and make up by far the largest proportion of members. Many seem to be content to play for the rest of their days with the swing they have been 'stuck' with. They should remember that it is never too late to learn, nor is it ever too late to improve. Men and women in their fifties and sixties can still give the young 'tigers' a good game if they set about making the greatest possible use of their potential and their individual physical capabilities. You are never too old to play better.

PRACTICAL PRACTICE

Whenever golfers get together, it is not long before the styles and techniques of the world's great players come under discussion and time and again I hear the question asked: 'Why is it that the Americans have such a commanding position in world golf today? Palmer, Casper and Nicklaus simply leave us standing.' Of course, it is not only the Americans who are proving themselves the outstanding players of today. Men like Gary Player, Bruce Devlin, Bruce Crampton, Harold Henning and Cobie Le Grange have all got a way with them too.

Watching the not-so-famous, but still quite promising, young American professionals at Royal Birkdale quite recently, it was interesting to see that, whenever they had a moment to spare, there they were on the practice ground trying to put their games in tip-top order. Many of them had not experienced this type of seaside golf before, but from dawn to dusk they stood on the practice ground trying to learn shots that would cope with these strange conditions as well as practising all the other shots in the bag. In addition to that they were playing two rounds a day in order to try to learn the course.

One hears a good deal about the so-called 'American method'. I think there is one, but it has nothing to do with style or action. Neither has it anything to do with the way they grip the club, their position at the top of the backswing, the way they bring the clubhead into the ball, or the finish of the swing. It seems to me that the American method is in the *mind*, and in the way they go about their business. On the practice ground there is no doubt that the Americans practise much harder than they are given credit for, and certainly much harder than anyone I have ever seen before. They also understand that to make the ball do what they want it to do, they have got to control the clubhead all the time. This is the essential difference between these fellows and those golfers who are simply trying to perfect their style. The American always has an object in mind and he is prepared to flog away on the practice ground to perfect that object.

Many young golfers try to ape these champions of the game, but often all they succeed in doing is copying their idiosyncrasies. They don't really get to the meat of these great players' styles because they don't feel the club in their hands and they don't know what objects their hero might have in mind.

Among the world's great players there always has, and always will be, a tremendous variation in styles. But the one thing that they all have in common is perfect control of the clubface through the hand action.

Not so long ago I asked a well-known international golfer for his views on the difference in standards between British and American golfers. He said that the varying weather conditions we have in Britain are not really conducive to the acquisition of a grooved repeating swing which is learnt by the Americans in warm still air, playing with the larger American ball on lush grass. Even the average club member on the other side of the Atlantic reckons to spend many pleasant hours on the practice ground where, at his ease and in safety, he can have a lesson or just hit shots without the bother of having to pick up the balls afterwards. Very few golf clubs in Britain can boast anything resembling this and I'm afraid that, at far too many clubs, practice grounds are non-existent. Assuming, however, that some kind of practice ground is available, it is up to the individual golfer to make use of it.

The international golfer went on to say that the wonderful performances of British players like Tony Jacklin, Ronnie Shade and Michael Bonallack could all be traced back to the hard work these fellows have been prepared to put in on the practice ground.

There is no doubt about it: if you want to get to the top of the golfing ladder you have to work as hard as the American boys do. They are absolutely dedicated, and every day they practise their driving, long-iron shots, approach shots, chipping and bunker play – but, most of all, they spend hours and hours on the practice putting green. It would drive an ordinary mortal almost insane to have to do this amount of work to get to the top, but these fellows seem to thrive on it and love being there. They know that eventually all this hard work must pay off and, when that happens, the rewards for a top professional will make it all seem worthwhile.

I was very impressed at Birkdale by a young man named Kermit Zarley, who practised for so many hours that I asked him: 'Don't you ever get tired of this?'

He replied: 'Yes, I get tired of it, but I enjoy it. When I start getting tired, I go and have a coffee, or I just walk around for a bit. Then perhaps I'll go out and play a few holes, and when I feel fresher I come back to the practice ground. If you want to get to the top, this is the only way to do it.'

Once you've 'arrived' it isn't so essential to keep practising all the time. In fact, nowadays, Palmer, Player and Nicklaus don't need to practise very much. All they have to do is maintain their form and this they can usually do simply by playing in a tournament. However, until you've 'got it', you just have to practise.

You may not have either the ability or the desire of a fellow like Kermit Zarley, but there's no doubt that every golfer would improve his game if he could spend more time on the practice ground. Over the years I've proved to myself that the golfers who practise are the ones who win competitions and get their handicaps down fastest. Even hitting balls into a net is good practice, as long as you concentrate on the swing and build up a good rhythm. If you are having lessons, net practice is very helpful until the changes you have had to make to your swing begin to feel more comfortable.

Too few players practise with a definite purpose in mind. Most people just seem to stand there and hit balls, one after the other, as fast as they can. Every shot is given the full treatment, and the predominant thought in the minds of these players is 'how *far* did I hit it?' and not '*how* did I hit it?'

There are three main points to remember when practising. First, you've got to practise to improve your swing. Most golfers have a clear mental picture of the swing they would like and which they feel fairly confident of achieving. For some, this swing will be long and flowing with a slow and deliberate rhythm. Others may lean towards a more compact and punchy action – an aggressive swing. It's up to every individual to discover for himself the best type of swing and the best way to hit the ball, and the best place to find that out is on the practice ground.

If you normally use a slightly open stance, why not try using a square, or even a closed, stance? You might find that either of these suit you better. If you normally swing with a slightly open clubface, don't be afraid of trying to hood the face on the practice ground.

So this is the second thing to remember: don't be afraid of experimenting. If you hit bad shots, they are doing no harm, but you might well discover that another method suits you better than the one you've been using for years.

The third point to remember on the practice ground is probably the most important. To play any golf shot well, the ball must be struck bang in the centre of the clubface which has been brought squarely into the back of the ball by the hands. Practice is the only way of becoming a good striker of the ball. You may be a good swinger, but only hitting golf balls regularly helps you to develop into a good striker – and from this you improve into becoming a good competitor.

Regular tuition is a 'must' for all weekend golfers who want to improve their game, and this goes for young professionals too. By having a lesson they could save themselves hours and hours of unnecessary hard work and worry trying to find what might turn out to be a very simple fault.

Any sort of practice is good practice, even though you may not hit the ball well all the time. As long as you try to hit the right shots, at least you will be building up the correct golfing muscles and, through perseverance, your game is bound to improve.

Few golfers practise as much as they should. Many seem to be a little bit afraid of practising what may be faults. If you feel like this, go to a professional and have a couple of lessons. It will eliminate the uncertainty of whether your swing is good or bad and it will give you the confidence to go away on your own and practise on the right lines.

When you go to the practice ground next time, say to yourself: 'I'm going to try something I haven't tried before and, in trying to improve my game, I'm going to seek the best method for me as an individual. And I'm really going to keep that clubface under control all the time.'

Many golfers – 'fair weather players' they are called – never take their clubs out of the locker during the winter. After a layoff like that, most of them are a little slow to take up the cudgels again because they are a bit apprehensive about the state of disrepair into which their game may have fallen.

I suggest that, after a long layoff, you return to the game with plenty of practice swinging sessions without a ball, first with the left hand, then the right and then both together. This will gradually get rid of the stiffness in the golfing muscles and it's surprising really how quickly the feel of the swing starts coming back.

This can be followed by one or two sessions at the driving range or on the practice ground and then you will be all set to go once again. I don't think that the average golfer ever really loses his swing, but if he hasn't played for a while his hands and feet feel very sluggish. He discovers that he isn't hitting the ball as far as he was last season and it takes a little time before he feels prepared to make the effort to snap the wrists as he comes into the shot.

Many golfers develop little exercises to help strengthen their hands: squeezing a squash ball is an old favourite. This is fine, and for youngsters who are really keen to build up their physical condition, cross-country running and weight training are both very good.

As far as I'm concerned, there's nothing better for golf than golf itself. The finest way of building up the strength in your hands is plenty of practice swinging without a ball and using a heavy club. Swing for a couple of minutes with one hand, then with the other and finally with both together. Ten minutes a day of this sort of routine can really work wonders on your game.

So many people don't have the time to go up to the golf club in the evenings and hit shots, but everybody can find the time to have a few practice swings in the garden. Apart from building your golfing muscles, this is a very good way of improving your style.

When Henry Cotton was in his prime, he was never without a short heavy club. It went wherever he went and he would swing it every spare moment. He realized the value of good strong hands in golf, and he appreciated that the stronger they were the more control he had over the ball and the faster he could hit through with the clubhead.

So many players swing the club very nicely and hit the ball well 150 yards down the middle. They will never hit the ball further than that until they develop a good, strong hand and wrist action. The only reason that Arnold Palmer hits the ball so far is that he is able to bring the clubhead through with lightning speed. If it travelled at the same speed as Mrs Jones's clubhead, he would hit the ball no further than Mrs Jones. It's as simple as that.

Only practice will develop your golfing strength, so if you want to become a better player, you are going to have to be prepared to devote some time to the practice ground.

PREPARING FOR A COMPETITION

Many players fail to produce their best golf when playing in competitions, and quite often the reason is because they do not understand the importance of good preparation. The advice I shall offer in this chapter is bound to be beneficial whatever your handicap, but it is absolutely vital to the young tournament player, whether he is an amateur or a professional.

First-class physical condition is a 'must' and I would encourage any reasonable exercise that will promote this. In particular, your hands, wrists and forearms must be in good shape, and you can do no better than plenty of practice swinging with a specially weighted club or the heaviest club in the bag. I don't know of any top-class player who hasn't got really strong hands, wrists and forearms.

For youngsters, press-ups, skipping and a certain amount of weight training are all very helpful, for they build up strength and stamina in all parts of the body. You may be playing in a tournament of four rounds over a championship length course and this means that there will be quite a lot of physical strain. For the weekend golfer, some practice swings or hitting shots just before you step on to the tee will help in limbering up and getting the feel of the various clubs. Most probably you haven't hit a ball since last Sunday, so it's up to you to get your hands into good condition, and practice swinging is the best way I know of doing it. If you live close to a driving range, it may be a good idea to pop in and hit a few balls – but be careful not to overdo it; you mustn't go to the tee feeling exhausted before you even start the round.

Always check your equipment carefully, making sure that

you have the correct number of clubs in the bag. The limit is fourteen clubs in any one bag, but it's easy either to leave one out, or for somebody accidentally to slip an extra club into your bag instead of his own. If you have more than the permitted number, you can be penalized.

If you use a left-hand glove to help you grip the club firmly, make sure that you are carrying a spare. If it starts pouring with rain, you will have a dry glove to wear after the first nine holes, say. This could save you a couple of strokes coming home.

Have several ball markers handy so that when you have to mark your ball on the green, you can get at the marker easily. They have an infuriating habit of hiding in the deepest recesses of your pocket and wasting time trying to find one could lead to a hurried putt.

The condition of the grips on your clubs is of the utmost importance, yet it is something that club golfers sadly neglect. If the grips are worn out, for goodness' sake have them replaced. It is well worth the expense. If they are in good order but have become shiny with use, rub them down with a little castor oil. This quickly restores the tackiness to leather grips. Rubber grips can be improved simply by scrubbing them in soap and water. Ideally, grips should feel easy to hold securely without having to grip too tightly. Arnold Palmer changes his grips every three or four months, and he's very fussy about the way he does it. Like Palmer, you can afford to take a little more care over this vital detail.

As to clothing, try to avoid wearing anything new – particularly things like shoes and waterproof jackets. To start with they can feel uncomfortable and, unless you feel your best, you are not likely to play your best. The great Harry Vardon once said: 'I would no more think of wearing a new pair of braces in a tournament than I would think of wearing a pair of new boots.'

New clubs also need a lot of knowing. They may look good, feel good, and fill you with confidence, but you shouldn't use them in a competition until you have got to know them very well. It takes many practice shots and many rounds of golf to appreciate fully the subtle differences between your new set and the set they have replaced.

When I was playing in tournaments, I used to take a tin of sweets or a bar of chocolate out on to the course with me. You may be out there for a long time, and a bite of chocolate can stave off any hunger pangs or settle you psychologically.

Keep a rule book in your pocket, remembering that a marker is not a referee and neither is the person you are playing with on the day of the competition.

Give yourself plenty of time before you are due to tee off. I have seen so many bad shots played on the first few holes simply because the player has rushed to the course and then dashed on to the tee without giving himself any chance to relax and limber up.

If you are travelling away from home to a tournament, I suggest that you stick to your normal bedtime, and keep as near as possible to your usual diet.

You may be lucky enough to have a caddie, but if you find after a few holes that he is unable to club you properly and can't read the greens accurately, don't dither – choose your own clubs and decide to take your own lines. You should know more about your game than he does. The days of the first-class caddie have long since gone; nowadays most of them are just bag-carriers and they are not very helpful when it comes to playing the shots, choosing the clubs or offering the right line on the green.

Play at least one practice round commencing at the same time as your starting time for the tournament. If you've got an early morning start, practice over the course in the early morning. Changes in light can easily upset your judgment of distances.

It's strange how few bunkers one gets into during a pre-tournament round. But when the competition starts they seem to have a habit of springing up overnight! Bunker shot practice is very important, and gives you the chance of testing both the depth and the texture of the sand. Even if you don't hit a ball into a bunker during your practice round, toss a couple of golf balls into a trap and hit them out. As long as you smooth the sand over carefully when you've finished, nobody will mind your doing this.

During the few days before a tournament starts, the flags are usually placed at the front of the greens to save the putting surfaces from wear and tear, but invariably on the day of the competition they will be at the back. Remember this when you are playing your practice rounds, and try to pitch the ball at the back of the green on every hole. Even if the flag is placed further forward once the tournament begins, at least you will have a good idea of what club to play.

Have a few practice shots from the rough round the greens. Sometimes this will be 'woolly', and it's a terribly difficult thing to decide how the ball will fly out of it. It's all too easy to get scared when the pressure is on and you might well fluff it, so get the feel of this grass and the resistance it offers the clubhead.

If possible, arrange to walk round with the favourite for the tournament and watch the way he plays his shots and copes with the various problems of the course. You can learn quite a bit. You will probably notice that he takes an iron off certain tees and a 3 wood at others, rather than risking trouble by using a driver. At some long holes he may decide to play a couple of iron shots short of the green and hope to get his birdie four with a pitch and putt.

If he's off earlier than you and you are watching him play on the actual day of the tournament, take particular notice of the pin placements. You might see, for instance, that the hole is placed at the back of the third green, but on the front edge at the fifth. This is invaluable information to possess when you come to play your approach shot, for you will know exactly what you are aiming for.

Most of the top players send their caddies out on to the course early in the morning after the holes have been cut for the day. The caddies then write the information down so that both they and their bosses know exactly where the flag is. This will help the good player to place his tee shot, for these fellows play the entire hole, not just the approach shot, with the pin position firmly in mind.

All this is simply good preparation for a tournament, and it doesn't only apply to the top-class players either. I think that it is just as important for the average club golfer to get himself properly organized, so that when the competition gets under way he is in good mental condition and he knows that he has left nothing to chance.

One must have almost unlimited patience and restraint when playing a round of golf. There are so many things that can easily upset one, but try not to let this happen to you. If the people in front are very slow, take things quietly and walk a little slower yourself. Don't get all het up and frustrated about it; learn to pace yourself. I remember watching Arnold Palmer relaxing during a round of golf that took nearly five hours. As soon as he stepped on to every tee, he made straight for the tee box and had a sit-down, and at every opportunity he had round the course he rested quietly. It's a great thing if you can do it during some of these long tough tournament rounds.

You may never play in any competitions more serious than your club's monthly medal, but everybody likes to be able to win, however slight the prestige may be. Give yourself every chance and get properly tuned up to play competitive golf.

IN CONCLUSION...

In this book, I have tried to set out as simply as possible what I believe to be the basic principles of golf. I have tried to make it easily understandable for everyone, with no distinction between men and women. The basics of good golf are the same for everybody, and while women may never have the physical strength of men, it is up to them to develop their hands as much as possible and use their physique to its greatest advantage.

This book can never be a substitute for personal tuition. Professional golfers have a trained eye and can soon pick out your particular faults and problems before you get lost in a fog of uncertainty. Your professional is not there simply to feather his own nest; he is there to give you a service and to help you enjoy golf to the full.

What I have said in this book should give you an overall impression of what you are trying to achieve and, if you already know your faults, it may help you to see them more clearly and explain how you can put them right.

There are many things that I haven't discussed, simply because this volume is aimed at the raw beginner and the long handicap golfer in particular, and I do not want to over-complicate the issue too much and confuse you. I want to give a clear mental picture of the golf swing and the importance of the hands in relation to the clubhead.

After forty years as a professional golfer, my one object is to give the masses of people who want to play golf as much enjoyment as I can. There is no doubt that the better you play, the more you will enjoy the game.

Golf is many things, It is a delightful walk in beautiful

surroundings, it is good company and fellowship, but most of all golf is *fun*. Don't ever forget that and become desperate or neurotic over the game. If you do, it would be better to hang your clubs up for good.

If I have helped you to improve your game, or if through these pages I have whetted your appetite sufficiently to try golf, I am well satisfied with my labours. I hope you enjoy reading them as much as I have enjoyed writing them. Good golfing!

APPENDICES

WHERE TO FIND YOUR GOLF

Below is a list of the public golf courses of England and Scotland, giving details of the charges per round, but it must be stressed that these costs are liable to change: with the modern trend, they are only likely to increase!

To assist you in finding a public course in your area, this list has been prepared under counties. Although municipal courses do not exist in Wales and Ireland, most private clubs welcome visitors on a green fee basis – although charges are generally rather higher than public courses.

Most municipal golf courses, particularly near densely populated areas, are invariably very busy, and starting times are allotted to those wishing to play. For this reason, it is usually worth while contacting the course manager well in advance of the time you want to play.

ENGLAND

Cheshire

Altrincham	Altrincham Municipal GC, 6,282 yards, 18 holes. Mon–Fri 7*s* 6*d*; Sat–Sun 12*s* 6*d*.
Birkenhead	Arrowe Park GC, 5,900 yards, 18 holes. Mon–Fri 3*s* 6*d*; Sat–Sun 5*s*.
Hoylake	Hoylake Municipal GC, 6,312 yards, 18 holes. Mon–Fri 5*s*; Sat–Sun 7*s*.
Wallasey	Warren GC, 5,914 yards, 9 holes. Mon–Fri 3*s* 6*d*; Sat–Sun 5*s*.

Derbyshire

Chesterfield	Chesterfield Municipal GC, 5,875 yards, 18 holes. Mon–Fri 4*s* 6*d*; Sat–Sun 6*s*.
Derby	Allestree GC, 5,638 yards, 18 holes. Mon–Fri 6*s*; Sat–Sun 8*s* 6*d*. Derby Municipal GC, 6,197 yards, 18 holes. Mon–Fri 6*s*; Sat–Sun 8*s* 6*d*.

Essex

Basildon	Basildon GC, 6,127 yards, 18 holes. Mon–Fri 7*s* 6*d*; Sat–Sun 10*s* 6*d*.
Brentwood	Brentwood Municipal GC, 5,600 yards, 18 holes. Mon–Fri 4*s*; Sat–Sun 6*s*.
Chingford	Chingford GC, 5,600 yards, 18 holes. Mon–Fri 4*s*; Sat–Sun 6*s*. Royal Epping Forest GC, 6,219 yards, 18 holes. Mon–Fri 4*s*; Sat–Sun 6*s*.
Chigwell	Hainault Forest Municipal GC, two courses of 6,445 yards and 5,754 yards, both 18 holes. Mon–Fri 7*s* 6*d*; Sat–Sun 10*s*.
Southend-on-Sea	Belfairs Municipal GC, 5,977 yards, 18 holes. Mon–Fri 6*s*; Sat–Sun £1.

Hampshire

Bournemouth	Meyrick Park GC, 5,860 yards, 18 holes. Mon–Sat 10*s*. No play on Sundays. Queen's Park GC, 6,635 yards, 18 holes. Mon–Sat 10*s*. No play on Sundays.
Portsmouth	Portsmouth Municipal GC, 6,000 yards, 18 holes. Mon–Fri 7*s* 6*d*; Sat–Sun 10*s*.
Southampton	Bassett GC, 6,163 yards, 18 holes, and 2,391 yards, 9 holes. Mon–Fri 2*s* 6*d*; Sat–Sun 4*s*.

Hertfordshire

Rickmansworth	Rickmansworth Municipal GC, 4,551 yards, 18 holes. Mon–Fri 5*s*; Sat–Sun 10*s*.
St Albans	Batchwood Hall Municipal GC, 6,465 yards, 18 holes. Mon–Fri 10*s*; Sat–Sun £1, but 10*s* for local residents.

Isle of Man

Douglas	Douglas Municipal GC, 5,859 yards, 18 holes. Any day of the week 4*s*.

Kent

Beckenham	Beckenham Place Park Municipal GC, 5,677 yards, 18 holes. Mon–Fri 7*s* 6*d*; Sat–Sun 10*s*.
Bromley	Bromley GC, 5,538 yards, 9 holes. Mon–Fri 3*s*; Sat–Sun 5*s*.
Eynsford	Lullingstone Park GC, 6,300 yards, 18 holes. Mon–Fri 5*s*; Sat–Sun 9*s*.

Lancashire

Blackpool	Blackpool Park GC, 18 holes, Mon–Fri 7*s* 6*d*; Sat–Sun 12*s* 6*d*.
Bolton	Bolton Municipal GC, 6,102 yards, 18 holes. Mon–Fri 4*s* 6*d*; Sat–Sun 7*s* 6*d*.
Bootle	Bootle Municipal GC, 6,148 yards, 18 holes. Mon–Fri 2*s* 6*d*; Sat–Sun 3*s* 6*d*.
Burnley	Towneley Park GC, 5,735 yards, 18 holes. Mon–Fri 4*s*; Sat–Sun 5*s*.
Liverpool	Allerton Municipal GC, 5,084 yards, 18 holes. Mon–Fri 3*s* 6*d*; Sat–Sun 4*s* 6*d*.
Manchester	Manchester Municipal GC, 5,840 yards, 18 holes. Mon–Fri 4*s* 6*d*; Sat–Sun 5*s* 6*d*.

Rochdale	Springfield Park GC, 9 holes. Mon–Fri 3*s* 6*d*; Sat–Sun 4*s* 6*d*.
Southport	Southport Municipal GC, 6,200 yards, 18 holes. Mon–Fri 5*s*; Sat–Sun 7*s* 6*d*.
Leicestershire	
Leicester	Western Park GC, 6,895 yards, 18 holes. Mon–Fri 5*s*; Sat–Sun 7*s*.
London	
Hanwell	Brent Valley Municipal GC, 18 holes. Mon–Fri 5*s*; Sat–Sun 7*s* 6*d*.
Richmond	Richmond Park GC, two courses of 5,971 yards and 5,925 yards, both 18 holes. Mon–Fri 6*s*; Sat–Sun 8*s*.
Wimbledon	Wimbledon Common GC, 5,416 yards, 18 holes. Mon–Fri 5*s*; Sat–Sun 15*s*.
Middlesex	
Enfield	Enfield Municipal GC, 5,500 yards, 18 holes. Mon–Fri 4*s* 6*d*; Sat 6*s*; Sun 7*s* 6*d*.
Greenford	Perivale Park GC, 5,200 yards, 9 holes. Mon–Fri 2*s*; Sat–Sun 3*s*. Horsenden Hill GC, 3,030 yards 9 holes. Mon–Fri 2*s*; Sat–Sun 3*s*.
Northwood	Haste Hill GC, 5,641 yards, 18 holes. Mon–Fri 7*s* 6*d*; Sat–Sun 10*s*.
Ruislip	Ruislip Municipal GC, 5,126 yards, 18 holes. Mon–Fri 7*s* 6*d*; Sat–Sun 10*s*.
Northamptonshire	
Corby	Priors Hall GC, 6,636 yards, 18 holes. Mon–Fri 5*s*; Sat–Sun 6*s*.
Northumberland	
Berwick-upon-Tweed	Magdalene Fields Municipal GC, 5,460 yards, 9 holes. Any day of the week 2*s*.

Newcastle-upon-Tyne	Westerhope Municipal GC, 6,383 yards, 18 holes. Mon–Fri 7*s* 6*d*; Sat–Sun 15*s*.
Nottinghamshire	
Nottingham	Nottingham GC, 6,284 yards, 18 holes. Mon–Sat 7*s* 6*d*; Sun 12*s*.
	Nottingham Municipal GC, 18 holes. Mon–Sat 7*s* 6*d*; Sun 12*s*.
Somerset	
Taunton	Taunton Municipal GC, 18 holes (par three). Mon–Fri 2*s* 6*d*; Sat–Sun 3*s* 6*d*.
Surrey	
Croydon	Addington Court GC, 18 holes and 9 holes; also a large practice area. Mon–Fri 4*s* 6*d*; Sat–Sun 7*s* 6*d*.
Esher	Thames Ditton and Esher GC, 5,415 yards, 9 holes. Mon–Fri 5*s*; Sat–Sun 7*s* 6*d*.
Kingston-upon-Thames	Home Park GC, 6,380 yards, 18 holes. Mon–Fri 6*s*; Sat 9*s*; Sun 14*s*.
Mitcham	Mitcham Common GC, 5,898 yards, 18 holes. Mon–Fri 5*s*; Sat–Sun 7*s*.
Coulsdon	Coulsdon Court Municipal GC, 5,982 yards, 18 holes. Mon–Fri 7*s*; Sat–Sun 12*s* 6*d*; but 8*s* for local residents.
Sussex	
Brighton	Hollingbury Park Municipal GC, 6,394 yards, 18 holes. Mon–Fri 7*s* 6*d*; Sat–Sun 10*s*.
	Waterhall GC, 5,213 yards, 18 holes. Mon–Fri 7*s* 6*d*; Sat–Sun 10*s*.
Seaford	Seaford Head GC, 5,942 yards, 18 holes.
Worthing	Hill Barn GC, 6,189 yards, 18 holes. Mon–Fri 7*s* 6*d*; Sat–Sun 12*s* 6*d*.

Warwickshire

Birmingham	Cocks Moors Woods GC, 18 holes. Minimum charge 5*s*. Harborne Municipal GC, 4,654 yards, 9 holes. Mon–Fri 5*s*; Sat–Sun 6*s*. Lickey Hills GC, 5,721 yards, 18 holes. Mon–Fri 5*s*; Sat–Sun 6*s*. Marston Green GC, 18 holes. Minimum charge 5*s*. Pype Hayes GC, 18 holes. Minimum charge 5*s*. Warley GC, 9 holes. Minimum charge 5*s*.
Sutton Coldfield	Boldmere GC, 6,078 yards 9 holes. Any day of the week 5*s*.

Worcestershire

Oldbury	Brand Hall GC, 5,749 yards, 18 holes. Any day of the week 5*s* 6*d*.

Yorkshire

Barnsley	Barnsley Municipal GC, 6,069 yards, 18 holes. Mon–Fri 5*s*; Sat–Sun 10*s*.
Bingley	Bingley St Ives GC, 6,391 yards, 18 holes. Mon–Fri 7*s* 6*d*; Sat–Sun 17*s* 6*d*.
Bradford	Bradford Moor Municipal GC, 5,700 yards, 9 holes. Mon–Fri 5*s*; Sat–Sun 10*s*. Phoenix Park GC, 9 holes. Mon–Fri 3*s* 6*d*; Sat–Sun 5*s*.
Hull	Hull Municipal GC, 6,415 yards, 18 holes. Mon–Fri 5*s*; Sat–Sun 6*s*. Sutton Park GC, 6,411 yards, 18 holes. Mon–Fri 5*s*; Sat–Sun 6*s*.

Leeds	Gotts Park Municipal GC, 18 holes. Mon–Sat 5*s*; Sun 6*s*. Middleton Park Municipal GC, 9 holes. Mon–Sat 5*s*; Sun 6s. Roundhay Park Municipal GC, 9 holes. Mon–Sat 5*s*; Sun 6*s*. Temple/Newsam Municipal GC. Two 18-hole courses. Mon–Sat 5*s*; Sun 6*s*.
Sheffield	Beauchief Municipal GC, 18 holes. Mon–Fri 4*s*; Sat–Sun 6*s*. Tinsley Park Municipal GC, 18 holes. Mon–Fri 3*s* 6*d*; Sat–Sun 5*s*. Shiregreen Municipal GC, 9 holes. Mon–Fri 2*s*; Sat–Sun 3*s*.
Wakefield	Wakefield City GC, 6,349 yards, 18 holes. Mon–Fri 5*s*; Sat–Sun 7*s* 6*d*.

SCOTLAND

Aberdeenshire

Aberdeen	Balnagask GC, 18 holes. Mon–Sat 3*s* 6*d*; Sun 4*s* 3*d*. Hazelhead GC, 5,943 yards, 18 holes; also 9-hole courses and a par-three course. Mon–Sat 4*s*; Sun 5*s*. King's Links, 6,185 yards, 18 holes. Mon–Sat 3*s* 6*d*; Sun 4*s* 3*d*.

Angus

Arbroath	Arbroath Municipal GC, 6,078 yards, 18 holes. Mon–Sat 7*s* 6*d*; Sun 10*s*.
Carnoustie	Championship Course, 7,252 yards, 18 holes. Mon–Fri 7*s* 6*d*; Sat–Sun 15*s*. Burnside Course, 18 holes. Mon–Fri 5*s*; Sat–Sun 15*s*.

Dundee	Caird Park GC, 6,273 yards, 18 holes. Mon–Sat 4*s*; Sun 6*s*.
Monifieth	Medal Course, 6,409 yards, 18 holes. Mon–Sat 6*s*; Sun 10*s*.
	Ashludie Course, 18 holes. Mon–Sat 5*s*; Sun 7*s* 6*d*.
Montrose	Medal Course, 6,401 yards, 18 holes. Mon–Sat 7*s*; Sun 7*s* 6*d*.
	Broomfield Course, 6,396 yards, 18 holes. Mon–Sat 7*s*; Sun 7*s* 6*d*.
Ayrshire	
Ayr	Belleisle Course, 6,531 yards, 18 holes. Mon–Sat 4*s*; Sun 10*s*.
	Seafield Course, 5,205 yards, 18 holes. Any day of the week 4*s*.
Girvan	Girvan Burgh GC, 5,202 yards, 18 holes. Mon–Sat 3*s* 6*d*; Sun 10*s*.
Irvine	Irvine Ravenspark Municipal GC, 6,462 yards, 18 holes. Mon–Sat 5*s*; Sun 15*s*.
Kilmarnock	Kilmarnock Municipal GC, 18 holes. Mon–Sat 4*s*; Sun 6*s*.
Troon	Darley Course 6,213 yards, 18 holes. Mon–Fri 5*s*; Sat–Sun 7*s*.
	Fullarton Course, 4,721 yards, 18 holes. Mon–Sat 3*s* 6*d*; Sun 5*s*.
	Lockgreen Course, 6,750 yards, 18 holes. Mon–Fri 5*s*; Sat–Sun 7*s*.
Banffshire	
Cullen	Cullen Municipal GC, 4,650 yards, 18 holes. Any day of the week 3*s*.
Dunbartonshire	
Clydebank	Clydebank Municipal GC, 5,128 yards, 18 holes. Mon–Sat 3*s*; Sun 4*s*.

Fife

Crail	Crail Municipal GC, 5,499 yards, 18 holes. Mon–Fri 7*s* 6*d*; Sat–Sun 12*s* 6*d*.
Kinghorn	Kinghorn Municipal GC, 5,134 yards, 18 holes. Mon–Sat 6*s*; Sun 7*s* 6*d*.
Kirkcaldy	Kirkcaldy Municipal GC, 6,477 yards, 18 holes. Mon–Sat 3*s*; Sun 4*s*.
Leven	Leven Municipal GC, 5,245 yards, 18 holes. Any day of the week 2*s* 6*d*.
St Andrews	Old Course, 6,936 yards, 18 holes. Mon–Fri 12*s* 6*d*; Sat £1. No Sunday play. Eden Course, 6,250 yards, 18 holes. Mon–Fri 6*s*; Sat 8*s* 6*d*; Sun 10*s*. Jubilee Course, 6,005 yards, 18 holes. Mon–Sat 3*s*; Sun 10*s*. New Course, 6,612 yards, 18 holes. Mon–Fri 6*s*; Sat 8*s* 6*d*; Sun 10*s*.

Lanarkshire

Glasgow	Alexandra Park GC, 9 holes. Mon–Sat 3*s*; Sun 4*s*. Deaconsbank Course, 18 holes. Mon–Sat 3*s*; Sun 4*s*. King's Park Course, 9 holes. Mon–Sat 3*s*; Sun 4*s*. Knightswood Course, 9 holes. Mon–Sat 3*s*; Sun 4*s*. Lethamhill Course, 18 holes. Mon–Sat 3*s*; Sun 4*s*. Linn Park Course, 18 holes. Mon–Sat 3*s*; Sun 4*s*. Littlehill Course, 18 holes. Mon–Sat 3*s*; Sun 4*s*.

	Ruchill Course, 9 holes. Mon–Sat 3*s*; Sun 4*s*.
Hamilton	Hamilton Municipal, 9 holes. Any day of the week 2*s*.
Lothians	
North Berwick	West Links, 6,323 yards, 18 holes. Mon–Fri 7*s* 6*d*; Sat–Sun 12*s* 6*d*. Burgh Course, 18 holes. Mon–Fri 7*s*; Sat–Sun 10*s*.
Dunbar	Winterfield Municipal GC, 4,262 yards, 18 holes. Any day of the week 6*s* 6*d*.
Edinburgh	Braids No. 1 Course, 18 holes. Any day of the week 3*s* 6*d*. Braids No. 2 Course, 18 holes. Any day of the week 3*s* 6*d*. Carrick Knowe Course, 18 holes. Any day of the week 3*s* 6*d*. Craigentinny Course, 9 holes. Any day of the week 3*s* 6*d*. Bruntsfield Course, (par three). Any day of the week 1*s* 6*d*. Inch Course, (par three). Any day of the week 1*s* 6*d*. Inverleith Course (par three). Any day of the week 1*s* 6*d*. Portobello Course, 9 holes. Any day of the week 3*s* 6*d*. Sighthill Course, (par three). Any day of the week 1*s* 6*d*. Silverknowes Course, 18 holes. Any day of the week 3*s* 6*d*.
Musselburgh	Musselburgh Municipal GC, 6,623 yards, 18 holes. Mon–Fri 7*s* 6*d*; Sat–Sun £1.

Peebles

Peebles	Peebles Municipal GC, 6,043 yards, 18 holes. Mon–Fri 6*s* 6*d*; Sat 7*s* 6*d*; Sun 12*s* 6*d*.

Perthshire

Perth	Perth North Inch Municipal GC, 5,141 yards, 18 holes. Mon–Sat 5*s*. No Sunday play.

Stirlingshire

Larbert	Falkirk Tryst Municipal GC, 6,037 yards, 18 holes. Mon–Sat 5*s*; Sun 10*s*.
Stirling	Stirling Municipal GC, 6,032 yards, 18 holes. Mon–Fri 6*s*; Sat–Sun 7*s* 6*d*.

DRIVING RANGES

Unlike the majority of public golf courses which are run by local authorities, nearly all the driving ranges in Britain have been opened by private enterprise during the last few years. But now councils are beginning to appreciate that golf centres and driving ranges are useful public amenities, and it may well be that during the next year or two we shall see more and more municipal driving ranges springing up.

Driving ranges vary from a few mats laid out on a piece of open ground to highly sophisticated centres, complete with heated and covered teeing bays, pitch and putt courses, putting greens, bars and restaurants. At most driving ranges, professional tuition is available, and it is recommended that the beginner arranges one or two lessons before trying to hit balls at a range – particularly if this is his first experience of the game.

Properly used, the driving range can be a boon to practice, but all too frequently, the customers' one intention is to try to hit the ball as far as they possibly can, with little regard for style, balance or rhythm. When you use a driving range, make sure that you think about each shot you play, and try to swing the club well.

The following list and details of golf driving ranges now open is complete at the time of writing, but readers should remember that more and more of them are being built each year.

Blackpool	John Jacobs Golf Centre, Fleetwood Road, Norbreck, Blackpool. A floodlit range with 25 tees, 15 covered. Also a putting green, a golf shop, restaurant and licensed bar. Professional tuition

available. Charges: 30 balls, 2*s* 6*d*; 60 balls, 5*s*, Mon–Sat 10 am–5 pm, 6 pm–10 pm, Sun 10 am–1 pm, 2 pm–5 pm, 6 pm–10 pm.

Cardiff — Arnold Palmer Golf Range, Pontcanna, Cardiff. Floodlit range with covered tees. Professional tuition and licensed refreshments available. Also Arnold Palmer 18-hole putting course. Charges: 25 balls, 3*s*; 50 balls, 5*s*. Open seven days, 10 am–10 pm.

Cobham — Fairmile Driving Range, Portsmouth Road, Cobham, Surrey. Floodlit range with 24 covered tees, target greens and practice bunker. Professional tuition available, and clubs are loaned free of charge. Licensed bar and restaurant, practice putting green. Charges: 30 balls, 3*s* 6*d*; 60 balls, 6*s*. Mon–Fri 10 am–10 pm, Sat–Sun 9 am–9 pm.

Croydon — Croydon Driving Range, Long Lane, Croydon, Surrey. Floodlit range with 48 tees (double tiered), putting course, licensed bar and restaurant. Car parking for 450. Professional tuition from Jimmy and Nancy Hitchcock. Charges: 30 balls, 3*s* 6*d*; 60 balls, 5*s*. No charge for loan of clubs. Open seven days, 9 am–10.30 pm.

Dublin — John Jacobs Golf Centre, Foxrock, Dublin. Situated in centre of Leopardstown racecourse. Floodlit range with 36 covered tees and 40 open tees, also

9-hole pitch and putt course and 9-hole par three course. Licensed bar. Professional tuition available. Charges: 30 balls, 2*s* 6*d*; 60 balls 5*s*. Hire of club, 6*d*. Open seven days, 10 am–10 pm.

Ealing — Ealing Golf Range, Rowdell Road, Northolt, Middlesex. Floodlit range with 36 covered tees, licensed clubhouse. Car parking for 200. Professional instruction available. Charges: 50 balls, 5*s*. No charge for loan of club. Open seven days, 10 am–10 pm.

Esher — John Jacobs Golf Centre, Sandown Park, Esher, Surrey. In centre of Sandown Park racecourse. Floodlit range with 33 covered and heated bays, and 30 open tees. Also pitch and putt course and 9-hole par three course. Fully licensed bars and restaurants. Resident professional John Jacobs, also full professional staff. Charges: Before 7 pm – 30 balls, 3*s* 6*d*; 60 balls, 6*s*. After 7 pm – 30 balls, 4*s* 6*d*; 60 balls, 7*s* 6*d*.

Fetcham — Riverside Club and Driving Range, River Lane, Fetcham, near Leatherhead, Surrey. Range *not* floodlit; 18 covered tees, putting green, chipping course. Professional instruction available. Licensed clubhouse, changing rooms, showers. Charges: 60 balls, 5*s*. Club loaned free of charge. Open seven days, 9 am to dusk.

Finchley	Finchley Golf Centre, 444 High Road, Finchley, London, N.12. Floodlit range with 24 covered bays, 30 open tees, putting course. Snack bar. Professional tuition available. Car parking for 300. Charges: 30 balls, 3*s* 6*d*; 60 balls, 5*s*. Open seven days, 9 am–10.30 pm. Club loaned free of charge.
Greenford	Greenford Golf Course and Practice Centre, Greenford Road, Greenford, Middlesex. Floodlit range with 40 covered tees, putting green and 9-hole par three course. Meals served in licensed clubhouse. Professional tuition available. Charges: 25 balls, 2*s* 6*d*; 50 balls, 5*s*. Club loaned free of charge. Open seven days 8 am–11 pm.
Hastings	Hastings Driving Range, Bulverhythe Recreation Ground, St Leonards-on-Sea, Hastings, Sussex. Range *not* floodlit. Play from 20 open bays. Changing rooms and car parking for 50. Charges: 55 balls, 5*s*. Open 1st April–30th September, 10 am–one hour before sunset.
Ipswich	Ipswich Golf Range, Suffolk Showground, Bucklesham Road, Ipswich, Suffolk. Range *not* floodlit. 15 covered bays, 20 open tees. Professional instruction available. Charges: 40 balls, 3*s* 6*d*; 60 balls, 5*s*. Open seven days 10 am–one hour before sunset.

Leicester	Arnold Palmer Golf Range, Melton Road, Leicester. Floodlit range with 22 covered bays and 16 open tees, putting course, 3 pitching greens and practice bunker. Meals served in licensed clubhouse. Professional tuition available. Charges: 25 balls, 3*s*; 50 balls, 5*s*. Open seven days, 10 am–10 pm.
Margate	Margate Driving Range, Palm Bay Recreation Ground, Cliftonville, Margate, Kent. Range *not* floodlit. 20 open tees, changing rooms. Professional tuition available. Charges: 55 balls, 5*s*. Open 1st April–30th September, 10 am–one hour before sunset.
Newcastle	John Jacobs Golf Centre, High Gosforth Park, Newcastle-upon-Tyne, Northumberland. Floodlit range with 30 covered bays and 20 open tees, 9 hole pitch and putt course, putting green, licensed bar and restaurant. Professional tuition available. Charges: 30 balls, 3*s* 6*d*; 60 balls, 5*s*. Mon 12.30 pm–10 pm, Tues–Fri 10.30 am–10 pm, Sat–Sun 10.30 am–10 pm.
Preston	Arnold Palmer Golf Range, Blackpool Road, Ribbleton, Preston, Lancashire. Floodlit range with covered tees. Professional tuition and licensed bar available. Also Arnold Palmer putting course. Charges: 25 balls, 3*s*; 50 balls, 5*s*. Open seven days, 10 am–10 pm.

Richmond	Richmond Driving Range, Athletic Ground, Richmond, Surrey. Range *not* floodlit. Open tees. Large car park. Professional tuition available. Charges: 40 balls, 3*s* 6*d*; 50 balls, 4*s* 6*d*; 60 balls, 5*s*; 70 balls, 6*s*. Mid-April–mid-September: Mon–Fri 10 am–one hour before sunset; Sat–Sun 9 am–one hour before sunset. Mid-September–mid-April: Mon–Fri as above; Sat 9 am–1 pm; Sun 9 am–one hour before sunset.
Sheffield	Arnold Palmer Golf Centre, Bradway Road, Sheffield 8. Floodlit range with 22 covered bays and 7 open tees, putting course, snack bar and licensed bar. Professional tuition available. Charges: 30 balls, 3*s*; 60 balls, 5*s*. Open seven days, 10 am–10 pm.
Surbiton	Surbiton Golf Range, Woodstock Lane, Chessington, Surrey. Range *not* floodlit. 40 open tees. Large car park. Professional tuition available. Charges: 35 balls, 2*s* 6*d*; 75 balls, 5*s*. Open seven days, 10 am to one hour before sunset. From 1st September to mid-April range closes at 12 noon on Saturdays.
Walton-on-Thames	Ken Adwick Driving Range, The Towpath, Walton-on-Thames, Surrey. Range *not* floodlit. 25 open bays, putting green. Large car park. Professional tuition available. Charges: 25 balls, 2*s* 6*d*; 50 balls, 5s. Club loaned free of charge. Open seven days, 10 am–one hour before sunset.

Wolverhampton	Three Hammers Golf Centre, Coven, near Wolverhampton, Staffordshire. Floodlit range with 14 covered tees, 18-hole par three course and putting green. Restaurant and licensed bar. Professional tuition available. Charges: 25 balls, 3*s*; 45 balls, 5*s*. Club hire 6*d*. Mon 5.30 pm–10 pm. Other six days: 9 am–10 pm.

GLOSSARY OF GOLF TERMS

Golf can be a confusing game to the newcomer, and non-golfers sometimes have a terrible time trying to understand a golfing conversation in which such things as 'birdies', 'pars' and 'hooks' keep cropping up. Here, for the new golfer, or even for the golf widow, is a glossary of the most common golfing terms.

Addressing the ball: The way in which one positions oneself to hit the ball, and also places the clubhead behind the ball.

Albatross: A score for the hole which is three under par for that particular hole.

Attend: The flagstick is attended when either the player's opponent or caddie holds it, ready to pull it out as the ball approaches.

Baffy: An old type of wooden club that was used for playing lofted shots. Nearest modern equivalent is the 4 wood.

Birdie: A score for the hole which is one under par for that particular hole.

Bisque: A handicap stroke which the receiver can take at any stage of the match.

Blaster: A heavy wedge with a broad sole used for short pitches from heavy rough, and particularly for bunker shots.

Bogey: Competition played against the par of each hole, taking strokes as in a match, with three-quarters of the difference between the player's handicap and the standard scratch score of the course.

Brassie: Also known as the 2 wood. It derives its name from the brass plate in the sole of the club. The driver usually has a white-metal plate.

Bulger: A wooden club having a pronounced convexity of the face.

Bunker: See *hazard.*

Bye: The holes remaining to be played after the main match has ended.

Caddie: A person who carries the golfer's clubs.

Caddie cart: see *trolley.*

Casual water: Any temporary accumulation of water or snow visible before or after a player has taken up his stance. The player may obtain relief by lifting and dropping the ball away from the casual water, but not nearer the hole, without penalty.

Chip: A delicate stroke played from just off the green. The object is to land the ball well short of the hole and then let it run up close.

Cock: The bend of the wrists on the backswing.

Cut: see *slice.*

Dead: A ball is said to be 'dead' when it lies so close to the hole that the putt is a 'dead certainty'.

Divot: A piece of turf cut from the fairway after the club has made contact with the ball.

Dormy, Dormie: A side is dormy when it is as many holes up as there remain holes to play. If a player is two up with two to play, he is 'dormy two'.

Draw: A controlled hook caused by imparting an anti-clockwise spin to the ball, making it drift slightly right to left.

Eclectic: A score for the round achieved by taking two or more cards and counting the lowest score at each hole.

Eagle: A score for the hole two strokes better than par.

Fade: A controlled slice caused by imparting a clockwise spin to the ball which makes it drift slightly from left to right.

Fairway: The mown portion of turf at each hole, excluding the putting green and teeing ground.

Featherie, Feathery: The earliest known golf ball in Britain, made from hide and stuffed hard full of boiled feathers.

Flagstick: A movable indicator with bunting attached, placed in the hole to show its position.

Flat: Descriptive of the head of a club lying at a more obtuse angle to the shaft than a club with an upright lie. Also, a position at the top of the backswing where the hands are low, probably no higher than the shoulders.

Foozle: A bad, clumsily executed stroke.

Fore: Warning cry to players ahead, probably contracted from 'Look out, afore!'

Forecaddie: An extra caddie employed to go forward to watch the flight of the ball. The rules limit players to only one caddie, and forecaddies may only be appointed by the committee in charge of a competition.

Fourball: A match in which four players each play their own ball, and the lower score of two partners is the side's score for the hole.

Foursome: In Britain, a team consisting of two players playing one ball by alternate strokes. In America, the word 'foursome' means a fourball, and a Scotch foursome denotes the two-ball foursome.

Green: Traditionally the whole course, and one still sometimes reads of a championship being played 'on the Green of the ....Golf Club'. Also refers to the putting green.

Greensome: A modified form of foursome in which both partners drive from each tee, and then select one of the two drives with which to complete the play of the hole, thereafter playing alternate strokes.

Gobbler: A long fast putt which is holed against all the odds.

Guttie: In its original form (about 1848) this was a smooth sphere of solid gutta-percha, heated and shaped in a mould. It flew badly until well dented and nicked by iron shots, and later models were hand-hammered to create this effect from the start. Still later, moulds were made with set patterns which greatly improved its aerodynamic qualities. It was replaced gradually by the rubber-cored ball, which was introduced to Britain in 1901.

Grooved swing: A swing is said to be 'grooved' when the player is secure in the knowledge that it will repeat whatever the pressures. It always travels in the same arc.

Hanging lie: A lie which compels the player to stand either higher or lower than the spot where the ball lies.

Hazard: Any bunker or water hazard. A bunker is an area of bare ground, often a depression, which is covered by sand. A water hazard is any sea, lake, pond, river, ditch, surface draining ditch or any other open watercourse (regardless of whether it contains water). A lateral water hazard is one that runs approximately parallel to the line of play and has been so defined by the Greens Committee.

Head: The business end of a golf club, which comprises a face, a neck, a toe, a sole, and a heel.

Hosel: The shank of iron clubheads into which the shaft is fitted.

Hook: A sharp and uncontrolled right to left flight of the ball.

Hitting across the ball: When the player 'throws' the clubhead from the top of the swing into an outside arc, and swings from outside-to-in. Usual result is a slice.

Hitting early: Uncocking the wrists too soon on the downswing.

Hitting late: Uncocking the wrists at the last moment on the downswing, so that the hands lead the clubhead at impact.

Hitting down: Swinging down on the ball so that the clubface strokes the ball before taking a divot out of the turf.

Hooded: The clubface is hooded when the player addresses the shot with his hands well ahead of the ball, thus reducing the normal loft of the face.

Holes up: Method of scoring in matches, now little used, by which the complete round is played and the winner is credited by the number of holes by which he is ahead at the finish.

Hole: Hole cut in the putting green into which the ball is played. It must be four and a quarter inches in diameter, and at least four inches deep. Otherwise, one of the eighteen holes on a regular golf course, comprising teeing ground, fairway, rough, bunkers and putting green.

Like as we lie: A term used to illustrate the fact that, with the balls in their present position, each side has played the same number of strokes.

Like, playing the: To play a stroke which makes your score the same as your opponent's.

Links: Descriptive of dunes linked by sandy hollows along the seashore on which all Britain's championship courses are situated. The term can only be applied to sandy seaside courses.

Loft: The degree to which the face of the clubhead is set back from the perpendicular. It varies from the straight face of most putters to the extreme loft of the wedge.

Medal: Stroke competition played at every golf club at least once a month. Medal play is synonymous with stroke play.

Odd, playing the: The act of playing a shot which will make your score for the hole one more than your opponent.

One off two: To win a hole from an opponent who has been leading by two holes.

Par: The par of the hole is the score that a scratchman would be expected to do that hole in, and is largely dependent on the length of the hole. Holes of up to 250 yards rate as par three; holes of 251–475 yards rank as par fours; holes of 476 yards and upwards are par fives.

Press: To try to hit the shot too hard, and thus usually mistime the stroke.

Push: To send the ball to the right side of the course in a straight line. Usually caused by hitting inside-to-out with an open face.

Pull: To send the ball in a straight line to the left side of the course, usually by swinging outside-to-in with a shut face.

Putt: A stroke played on the green which sends the ball rolling towards the hole.

Roller: A player who rotates his wrists clockwise on the backswing, and anti-clockwise on the follow-through.

Rub of the green: Any interference by an outside agency to a ball in flight, after which the ball must be played where it lies.

Rubber-core ball: The ball universally used for golf. Made by winding rubber thread round a core and encasing the whole in a cover made either from vulcanised rubber or composition. First designed by Coburn Haskell in America, and introduced into Britain in 1901.

Sand wedge: Broad-soled, extremely lofted club, specifically designed for bunker play.

Sclaff or scruff: To hit the turf behind the ball, rather than hitting the ball before the turf. Also called 'hitting fat' and 'hitting heavy'.

Slice: A sharp and uncontrolled flight of the ball from left to right, often caused by coming across the ball from out to in with an open clubface.

Spoon: A wooden club with a fair degree of loft, used for hitting long shots with height. Both the 3 and 4 woods are called spoons.

Square: A player who does not rotate his wrists when playing the stroke.

Stableford: A form of competition devised by Dr Frank Stableford in which points are scored for the number of strokes at each hole. One point is scored for a hole completed in one worse than par, two for a par, three for a birdie, etc.

Standard scratch score: The basis for all handicapping, and is the course rating on any given day, taking into account the weather conditions and particular difficulties. The S.S.S. is allotted according to the overall length of the course, but it can be increased by the committee during a competition if, for instance, the wind is contrary at a par four hole and it is not possible to reach the green in two strokes. A player beating the S.S.S. of the day is likely to have his handicap decreased, even though the S.S.S. may have been higher than the figure allotted to the course.

Tee markers: Boxes, pyramids, plates or other prominent objects used to define the forward limits of the teeing ground.

Tee pegs: Wooden, plastic or rubber pegs on which the ball is placed for the drive.

Texas wedge: American term for a stroke played with a putter from off the putting green.

Takeaway: The first couple of feet of the backswing. A 'one-piece takeaway' is one where the arms, hands, and clubhead all travel back from the ball as one unit.

Top: A shot where only the top half of the ball is hit with the sole of the club. The usual result is that the ball scuttles along the ground for only a few yards.

Threeball: A game in which three players each play their own ball, and each plays the other two on a match-play basis.

Through the green: Any part of the hole except the teeing ground, hazards and putting green.

Trap: American term for a sand bunker.

Trolley: A wheeled contrivance for carrying the player's clubs.

Upright: Either the upright angle between the shaft and the clubhead, or the position at the top of the backswing. An upright position is one in which the hands are high above the shoulders.

Waggle: A gentle back and forth movement of the clubhead preparatory to making a stroke. Widely used to loosen the hands and wrists.

Wedge: A heavy lofted club with a wide sole which can be used either for a high approach shot or a low stopping shot with plenty of backspin.

Winter rules: Local rules not recognized by the rules of golf, but instituted by club committees to preserve the turf under winter conditions. It permits the player to move the ball to a better lie by rolling it with his clubhead. Also known as 'preferred lies'.